BEAUTIFUL DISASTERS

A FAMILY'S JOURNEY THROUGH TEEN DEPRESSION

CAROLYN C. ZAHNOW

Published by Motivational Press, Inc.
1777 Aurora Road
Melbourne, Florida, 32935
www.MotivationalPress.com

Copyright 2017 © by Carolyn C. Zahnow

All Rights Reserved

No part of this book may be reproduced or transmitted in any form by any means: graphic, electronic, or mechanical, including photocopying, recording, taping or by any information storage or retrieval system without permission, in writing, from the authors, except for the inclusion of brief quotations in a review, article, book, or academic paper. The authors and publisher of this book and the associated materials have used their best efforts in preparing this material. The authors and publisher make no representations or warranties with respect to accuracy, applicability, fitness or completeness of the contents of this material. They disclaim any warranties expressed or implied, merchantability, or fitness for any particular purpose. The authors and publisher shall in no event be held liable for any loss or other damages, including but not limited to special, incidental, consequential, or other damages. If you have any questions or concerns, the advice of a competent professional should be sought.

Manufactured in the United States of America.

ISBN: 978-1-62865-402-8

CONTENTS

FOREWORD 5

A BRIEF BACKGROUND 7

2001 - 2002 FRESHMAN 10

2002 - 2003 SOPHOMORE 34

2003 - 2004 JUNIOR YEAR 56

2004 - 2005 SENIOR YEAR 93

CAMERON IS AN ADULT NOW 140

AUGUST 11, 2005 159

REGRETS, WISHES, AND RECOMMENDATIONS 174

DISCOVERIES AFTERWARD 182

FROM CAMERON'S FRIENDS 185

RESOURCES 189

FOREWORD

I HAVE WRITTEN AN account of my son's life, from the period of his birth father's death to his own death at the age of 18. It is painful for me to remember those three years, but especially the day of Cameron's death.

There is nothing I would do differently if I could have a "do-over" during that time period, and even if I did, I'm not sure what we would have done. However, having hindsight is powerful, so I'm sure I would have learned more about grief and how a teen would react to a death. I would have been proactive in getting him into a support group, not just a new therapist every 6 months.

I'd like to thank my family members who have helped me on this journey of recovery. My husband Dan who was in the trenches with me the whole time, my mom and dad, my siblings – Kristie, who was especially sensitive to my raw emotions, and reminded me that journaling was a good idea (and probably saved me), Angela, Jacque and Tony who didn't know this was going on at the time, but supports me now.

There are also Cameron's closest friends who have allowed me to use their names in order to share this story of loss. I wish nothing but happiness for them as they endured the loss of a true friend in 2005. Love and hugs to Lauren, Kelly, Zach, Everett, Chris, and Amy.

I also thank all the supporters and attendees of The Shore Grief Center's grief support groups. They have helped me even though they don't realize it.

Carolyn Zahnow, 2017

A BRIEF BACKGROUND

BEAUTIFUL DISASTERS IS the follow up book to *Save the Teens*, published in 2010. *Save the Teens* explained teen depression, substance abuse, and suicide, among other teen type topics. I researched all the topics that confused me after my son's death by suicide. After moving back to North Carolina, I found that I had enough material to write a book, so I did.

In this book, I share events that happened from when my son's father died until his own death in 2005. It was a fast spiral down but it seemed to last forever at the same time.

First, some of the family dynamics:

Jace Cameron Stephenson was born on May 29, 1987. His father, J.C. Stephenson and I were married for 13 years. J.C. was a musician and sometime while I was pregnant, he became involved with one of his fellow band members (a younger woman). He was on the road often, so the opportunity was there.

He ultimately left me for her when Cameron was 3 months old. This was a dreadful position to be in and I kept it a secret from my family and friends for almost a year. I felt guilty for him leaving Cameron and I and thought it must have been my fault.

J.C. still wanted to be a father to Cameron so we set up a visiting schedule. Once Cameron was about 2 years old, we did the every-other-weekend visits. I would meet J.C. halfway, in Rocky Mount, on a Friday and would retrieve Cameron on Sunday afternoon.

When Cameron was about to start 1st grade, I enrolled in NCSU full time so I could get a good education and a better paying position to support my son with . I already had an AA degree, so earning a BA would not take too long – or so I thought.

I decided it would be good for Cameron to be with his dad more, so I offered to let him live with J.C. and his new wife, Nannette. By then they had a daughter, so Cameron also had a half-sister to play with. That was a good experience for all until J.C. started seeing another woman. After that happened, he moved to Battleboro to live with a good friend, and took Cameron along. I heard later that the living conditions were not great. J.C. eventually moved back in with his wife, as did Cameron.

It was when I decided to return to college that I met my husband and he was a great support for me. We were married in 1997 and Cameron came to live with us in 1998, in Raleigh.

Unfortunately, Dan lost his job and we had to move to Texas the following year for another job. Cameron was not happy about this move but ultimately made many good friends.

Cameron's dad had suffered from melanoma for several years and died when Cameron was 14, almost 15, years old. This was when the downslide started.

Cameron became depressed, irritable, lazy, and unpredictable – all signs of a grieving teen. We tried to save him from every angle but in the end, nothing saved his life.

I hope you'll take away a glimmer of what it's like to live with a depressed teen after reading *Beautiful Disasters*. I also encourage you to act faster than we did if you see signs of depression in your child, or yourself, and if grief is involved, please search out a support group or a grief therapist.

Thank you for reading our story.

2001-2002 FRESHMAN

THE THREE OF US SETTLED down in Texas and made our way - pretty much. Cameron made some great friends, which made living here much better for him. He does have a knack for making friends easily, same as his dad. However, neither of them seemed to make strong bonds with many friends, just a select few.

Cameron was still somewhat chunky but a happy teen and he'd pretty much do as he was told. He loved to play soccer and we kept him involved in the game since he enjoyed it.

Cameron's dad, J.C., got Cameron started in soccer when he lived with him in Bear Grass. J.C. even became the coach on the team Cameron played on! This was surprising as he was never the athletic type - J.C. was a musician!

Dan and I went to all the soccer games no matter where they were. Cameron didn't seem to give it his all but he enjoyed the camaraderie with the other guys.

Cameron enjoyed playing video games, like most teen boys, and was an avid gamer. His gaming partners were Everett and Chris. They would get together whenever possible, sometimes at our house, sometimes at Chris' house, but always on Friday nights at Everett's house.

Music was becoming more and more important to him, and his dad even shipped him a guitar, so Cameron was learning how to play. I had already given him the guitar I got when I was in high school but never learned to play. He liked to noodle around on the guitar, yet he was never interested in taking lessons. I assumed his dad taught him some chords on his visits back to North Carolina.

Cameron also decided that having a hamster was a great pet. Of course, he was not fond of cleaning out the cage so from time to time he received help from me.

Cameron didn't mind going on trips with Dan and I, or even going out to eat. Dan's hobby is cars so we took him along to car shows in the past, and he seemed to enjoy looking at the classic cars.

AUGUST 2001

Before school started, the three of us took a weekend road trip to Milwaukee, Butler, to be precise, to pick up some furniture that Dan's mother was giving us. She was selling her house and downsizing before moving into an apartment. It was a good trip for us.

On August 11, 2001, I made sure we took a side trip to one of Abraham Lincoln's formal homes and burial site in Springfield, IL. While I got the chills being in Lincoln's presence, the guys didn't get the significance of being there. Our past great president and his family were buried right where we were standing! I suppose I'm more sentimental and intuitive than most.

We also visited with Dan's brothers and their wives and kids. His mom loved seeing all of us again. However, we only stayed a couple of nights because Cameron had to start school that week.

2001 - 2002 Freshman

Cameron started his freshman year at Marcus High School in Flower Mound. Marcus is a big school, even sprawling in size. I always needed Cameron to go with me when I went to Open Houses so he could help me find where his classes were located. In order to prepare Cameron for the magnitude of Marcus, he attended "Fish School", which was to acquaint freshmen with the school before classes started.

SEPTEMBER 2001

Cameron started seeing a girl at school, Amy. They became very close and she seemed to teach him all her bad tricks, such as sneaking out of the house late at night, smoking pot, and who knows what else.

When Cameron had a sleep over, Everett and Chris came over and they would play video games all through the night. Since Cameron's room was upstairs, we hardly heard them at all when we were downstairs watching TV. The game room was a few short steps from Cameron's room. This was part of the reason I thought this house would be ideal for our family; Cameron could command most of the upstairs without us interfering. In hindsight, it probably was not the best idea.

Cameron was on the newspaper staff at school and had to learn how to take good pictures. As he didn't have a driver's license yet, I drove him around for different assignments. During this time, I actually learned how to take better pictures as well. We practiced "framing" by standing at the top of a hill and shooting down among some trees. Cameron didn't really like these assignments – he wanted to be more creative.

2001 - 2002 Freshman

The photo album I created of his photography shows that he managed to find beauty in everything he took a picture of; there are pictures of goats, frogs, friends skateboarding, farmers and shoppers at the Dallas Farmers Market, shopping carts, a highway overpasses, and a little girl in a pumpkin patch. So many types of scenes and images, all creatively shot.

For a glimpse into Cameron's brain at this point in his life, I'll share what he wrote about September 11:

> I arrived at school late that day because my alarm clock was screwed up. I was sitting in front of school as I normally do before school starts. Then this girl comes up and tells me and my friends that a plane flew into one of the twin towers. Of course we thought it was a joke. We thought that she may have had a little too much to drink the night before. So we just sat outside as if nothing happened.
>
> Then the bell rang so we all went inside and split in different directions to go to our first period classes. I had art at the time. So I went inside the art room and everyone was out of their seats watching the television. I asked Corey, he sat next to me, what was going on. He told me that a plane flew into one of the twin towers. It's strange because I didn't really have a reaction. More surprised than anything. So we didn't do anything that class period. We just watched the plane fly into the tower over, and over, and over again. I do remember watching it thirty or forty times in that one week alone.

So first period ended and we went on with second period. Then about third period, we heard that another plane had hit the other tower. Then they made it official that the crashes were not an accident. Sometimes reporters don't think before they talk. Seems like people would be able to figure out that two planes flying directly into the twin towers wouldn't be an accident. Especially if it was in the same day. That day pretty much consisted of nonstop watching the television for latest news.

That's how the day went. And hundreds of people died that day. All it took were two planes, terrorists, and corporate America to kill hundreds of people. In just one day. One very long day. That's what happened on September 11 in my life.

Cameron explained his taste in music in the same paper as the 9/11 paper...

This year my whole taste in music has completely changed. At the beginning of the year I heard about this band called System of a Down. I bought their new cd and had their old one burned. That started a whole revelation of heavy music. I got into Marilyn Mason, Godsmack, Korn, and Mushroomhead. A little later, I met a guy name Tyler. He was a punker. I had never really listened to punk because I never really heard about it. He let me listen to one of his Guttermouth cd's. I liked them somewhat. He told me about The Dead Kennedys. I had heard their Rawhide song and liked it a lot, so I went and bought my first Dead Kennedys cd. It was weird. I remember listening to them all the time. So then I decided to try another punk band. And after that, another. It kept growing and still hasn't ceased. Now pretty much all I listen to is punk. I'm glad that I met Tyler and he introduced me into it. Otherwise I might still be listening to Blink 182 and Eminem. Those were the embarrassing days. Now I listen to such bands as: Dead Kennedys, NoFx, Anti-Flag, The Vandals, The Clash, Rancid, Dropkick Murphys and The Descendants. There are more but those are my favorites. The reason I like punk so much is that it's all strong minded people that aren't afraid to say what they think. Most bands that I listen to have showed me what I think might not be what it really is. And for that I'll will always remember freshman year because of the music I was taught.

OCTOBER 2001

As Cameron had never experienced camping, I arranged for the three of us to go to Caddo Lake in east Texas for a weekend.

We pitched a 3-man tent that wasn't hard to put up and for dinner we grilled hotdogs at the campsite, we were roughing it.

When it came time for bed, Dan and I slept on an air mattress and Cameron was toughing it out in a sleeping bag. We were comfortable enough but we were not prepared for the rain that night. We got up the next morning and when we touched the roof of the tent, from the inside, water started seeping in! It was miserable.

Cameron and I got up early and crawled into the truck to warm up and dry out. Later, we took down the soaked tent, put away all the wet stuff, and got ready for our boat tour. We would have packed up and gone home, but we were looking forward to a tour of the lake that was full of creepy looking cypress trees with Spanish moss draped from limbs. I took some fun pictures while on the small boat they're priceless!

Caddo Lake is the only natural lake, or cypress swamp, in Texas, which is amazing because there are so many lakes in that huge state! Fortunately, it became a state protected park in 1931, which saved the uniqueness of the lake.

After our boat tour, we headed home. We were wet but happy from the experience.

NOVEMBER 2001

November was the month when our car club, Top Tin, held its annual car run, The Goat Roast. We were active in the club so we had several items to do for the event. We took Cameron along since he was still doing things with us and he was a bit too young to leave at home for a whole day.

He brought along Amy, his girlfriend and they cavorted around the small town of Muenster taking pictures to give them something to do while cars were coming. I asked Amy and Cameron to help selling Car Cards, this was a greeting card business I started earlier in the year.

They seemed to have had a good time at the car show, and

Amy took one of my favorite pictures of Cameron in Muenster that day. He's looking up at her and he has a burgundy string tied around his neck. He has a very sweet, angelic look on his face.

Overall, I don't think Amy was the best influence for Cameron. They were smoking cigarettes and pot when they would sneak out of their respective houses. She could persuade Cameron to do almost anything – or so it seemed.

DECEMBER 2001

I got a job at Nokia Mobile Phone Headquarters in Irving that December, which opened up lots of opportunities for me. I was able to attend ballet performances, opera and symphony concerts in both Dallas and Fort Worth. I was often able to get free tickets by volunteering at concerts.

This time though I bought tickets to go see The Nutcracker Suite for the three of us, but Dan had to be out of town on business, so I asked Cameron if he wanted to invite someone. He invited his friend Everett to join us and it was interesting watching these two high schoolers enjoying the ballet. It was held at Bass Hall in Fort Worth, which became my favorite place for performances.

We always asked Cameron to give us a list of what he'd like for Christmas. This was what he gave us that year:

Cameron's ChRiStMaS LIsT (as he typed it) –

Nightmare Before Christmas cd

Any of the cds that were ordered

Minidisk player ~ Sony is probably the best

Another rat fink guy

A hippopotamus

Deftones jacket .=from Hot Topic=.

Whatever else you guys think I might like

-Cameron 2001

Ok. That's what I would like for Christmas. I've pretty much been a good boy this year. Well.... Merry Christmas! Ok bye.

***

Christmas morning I continued a tradition my mom started when I was an adult. She would put together a hunt for a gift at the end. Cameron always enjoyed the thrill of the hunt and finding his gift. Of course, it required lots of work on my part the night before, coming up with hints where the next hint would be and finding an obscure place to hide his gift.

That Christmas it was HUGE gift – a pool table in the game room! Since it was outside Cameron's room, I doubt it was too much of a surprise. Dan and Cameron enjoyed shooting a game every now and then; and Cameron would also play with his friends when they came over. That was a great gift that could unite the boys.

Over the Christmas holidays, we set up a schedule for Cameron to visit his dad. One year he would stay with us for Christmas day and the next year he would go to his dad's house. This year, he was with us but the next day he headed to North Carolina.

After we moved to Texas, Dan and I decided not to fly to our families' houses each year but rather we would visit both in alternating years. I enjoyed that frantic travel – it was fun to me.

Cameron flew to North Carolina on a regular basis and there were no problems since it was a non-stop flight from DFW to RDU. He had become a pro at flying and I even got him an American frequent flyer card!

JANUARY 2002

All was well in the Zahnow/Stephenson household. I was plotting a family trip to London for my birthday in March. Our passports arrived and Dan was stunned even though I already told him about the trip.

Upon seeing the passports for Cameron and I,

Dan said, "I guess you're serious about this trip."

"Yep. I've bought our air tickets to London as well as found a hotel in London near the subway."

"What are the dates again? I need to be sure to take off from work."

"We leave on Thursday and return on Sunday. It's a short trip but it'll be fun. And I'll be there on my birthday!"

"All right then."

My anticipation grew but Cameron didn't seem to care one way or the other, I think he was dreading the long flight. Dan upgraded us so we were able to watch movies on the way over as well as have more room to stretch out.

FEBRUARY 2002

Cameron designed a Valentine's Day card on the computer for me, he typed "Remember: love isn't something celebrated one day a year. I luv you!" It had an elephant on the front and he drew a rose on the facing page. Sweet kid ☺

MARCH 2002

It was time to head to London! This was a dream of mine for a long time. Our trip was wonderful, at least in my eyes. It was a bit soggy as it rained every day at some point.

One of my goals was to have tea and scones at the Orangery at Kensington Palace on my birthday and that goal was achieved, even if we had to walk through a cold rain to get there that afternoon. Everywhere we went while on our trip, we walked and took the subway..

It was so cool to sit in the Orangery that was previously a huge English greenhouse, sipping tea with my two guys. I didn't mind the rain much and the guys couldn't complain because it was my birthday after all.

We also toured Kensington Palace, which is where many royals have lived, such as Princess Diana and Prince Charles. In the basement was an exhibit of the many gowns Diana wore during her time living at the palace. The guys really didn't care about seeing this exhibit.

Cameron enjoyed the trip even though he rarely showed it. Since he was 15, almost 16, he wanted to keep his distance from us, the parental units. He mostly wanted to "hang out" in central locations to look for "punkers and goth-types." However, I am a focused traveler and had every day planned out for us, we only had four days and I wanted to see it all!

I did slow down my touring madness so Cameron could enjoy it more . A couple of years later he admitted that he wanted to return to London and shoot photos.

We also visited London Tower – both of my guys really liked touring there. My favorite part was seeing the Crown Jewels. I bought a garnet necklace while there. They liked the horror that was attached with the tower – the beheadings, hangings, and such.

One day, we caught a train and went to Windsor to visit the Queen's castle. Cameron zipped through the castle and we found him outside sitting on a bench people watching, he had grown tired of touring old places by then.

We loved to explore at night as well. Big Ben was beautiful at night. Our evening meals were mostly eaten in pubs. I loved the fish and chips and Cameron discovered some type of stuffed potato and had that most nights.

On our flight home, we planned an extended layover in Raleigh so we could see family, and we saw most of everyone. That was a nice break from the long flight.

Some of Cameron's description of the trip included:

> It was pretty interesting. It was about as close to hell as I'll ever be while I'm alive I'm sure. England was beautiful. But I was stuck there for 4 days with my parents.
>
> It rained every day. But I didn't mind because I was on a constant sugar high. The biggest down about

the whole trip was the trip itself. The plane ride took forever and it became really annoying really fast. But England was fun but I still wish I had more time and less things to do.

***

We made it home and listened to our voicemail messages. There were a couple from Nannette, my ex's wife. She said that J.C. was in the hospital and we needed to get there as soon as possible, back in North Carolina.

J.C. had malignant melanoma and was fighting an inoperable brain tumor. I did not realize this was "the" phone call since I was not kept up to date on the ups and downs of J.C.'s illness.

Fortunately, it was still Cameron's spring break so he would not be missing any classes. I was able to find a weekend air special from Dallas to Virginia Beach; this was close enough to drive to Washington, N.C. where J.C. was in the hospital.

Jon, Dan's friend, offered to let Cameron and I stay at his river condo in Washington so we were set for a place to stay. Back from a long flight from Europe, we re-packed for a visit to North Carolina and then Cameron and I were off again. Dan stayed home and got back to work.

We arrived in the evening and while Cameron slept hard in the passenger seat, I had a long drive listening "The Clash" over and over again, because it was dark and a rental car, so I didn't know how to eject the CD!

We found the gated community of our friend's condo only to find out we couldn't get in the gate! I tried to call Jon but my cell phone didn't work in that part of the state – especially in the boonies. We waited until someone came out of the gate and we snuck in under the raised arm.

I remember that the Academy Awards were on that night so I tried my best to stay awake to watch them,. I do recall that Halley Berry won best actress. After that, I made my way to bed and collapsed. All that traveling did us in.

The next morning we arrived at the hospital in Washington and found the family, which began the next couple of days of hospital visiting. I saw my ex-husband briefly here and there when his wife was out of the room. I did get a chance to tell him that I loved him, for I did.

J.C. and I met while in high school. He was the new kid and quite a flirt. We actually met in the smoking area outside (Yes, the high schools caved and let us smoke on school grounds during 1973. Can you believe it?).

Jim, as he was known back then, was a senior and I was a junior. We dated casually the remainder of that school year and then he headed off to college in Florida. Turns out he moved there because he was in a relationship with an older lady. He was also secretly writing to another girl at our high school while courting me long distance. Quite the scamp, eh?

We finally got together for good after I graduated from high school in 1975. We married the next year while I was 19 and he was about to turn 20.

I loved J.C. since I was 17 years old and here he was in a hospital bed at the age of 45 surviving on oxygen, going in and out of consciousness, and under the influence of morphine to ease his pain. I had known and loved this man for 28 years!

I lost Alison, a very close girlfriend, five years previously to cancer. What was going on? Now I was about to lose another good friend, the father of my only child - my confidante in how to best raise our child.

Cameron was very stoic while at the hospital. His half-sister, Julia, was there for him to entertain, which he enjoyed. Julia is only two years younger than Cameron and she idolized her big brother. I have a fantastic photo of the two of them that I took outside the hospital. It's very ironic to see their smiling faces;I don't think they realized the severity of the occasion either.

I did not realize that J.C .was about to lose his battle with cancer until Monday morning, when we went back to the hospital to say our goodbyes.

I felt like I needed to get my son back home so he could return to school, but Nannette informed me that it wasn't a good idea. I was baffled. A nurse asked me to step inside the family room (where we stayed while visiting) and I was surrounded by three of J.C.'s doctors.

One doctor proceeds with, "Mrs. Zahnow, I'm afraid Mr. Stephenson is not doing well. The family would prefer that your son stay here. We feel that Mr. Stephenson will die very soon."

I was floored that I was corned like this, and stated, "I'm sorry but I did not know that he was dying as no one shared that with me."

"Yes, he is not well off. The family thinks it would be best for your son to stay."

I understood, but had wished someone had confronted me earlier. I didn't know that he was in the final stages of life. They must have assumed that I knew but how could I have known that?

I don't see dying people every day nor did they keep me informed of how sick he was. J.C. was in and out of hospitals over many years and I didn't know that this was his final trip.

I remember feeling at odds with the whole situation but agreed because, how do you argue with a family that has already started mourning?

I left my son there to be with his father while he took his final breath, just after midnight. I flew back to Texas and got word the following day that J.C. passed away.

Dan made arrangements for the two of us to fly back to North Carolina for the visitation and funeral. I was very happy Dan took on this chore, as I was stunned by the whole event.

During the visitation and funeral, Cameron hardly spoke to us. This was similar to driving a stake through my heart, since I so wanted to hold my son who was the creation of two people, of which one was now gone.

However, he kept his distance from us. My mom and sisters came to the funeral to provide moral support for us. J.C. was, after all, a member of my family for 13 years and the father of their grandson and nephew.

Cameron agreed to come back to our hotel and stayed with us after it was all over. He almost seemed relieved to be away from all the reminders that his dad was gone.

One of J.C.'s old friends was having a memorial at a bar the next night and wanted us to attend, but I felt a bar was not a place for Cameron to be. He seemed eager to go home anyway and had his own friends whom he, no doubt, missed seeing for the past two weeks.

We flew back home the next morning.

I found out years later, that Cameron remained angry with me for trying to get him to leave the hospital while his dad lay dying. He would not listen to my reasoning, which was a lack of information and communication.

I feel he was fed lots of misinformation from his stepmom, who always held a grudge against me. I'm not sure why since J.C. left me when our son was three months old in order to be with her.

Therefore, Cameron's spring break during his freshman year at high school, put simply, "sucked." Losing his dad was the worst thing that happened to him during his lifetime. One of Cameron's writings states that he lost his best friend that year.

Along with the joy in his life.

After J.C.'s death, I found myself wanting to pick up the phone, call J.C., and ask what to do about a Cameron issue, which was generally misbehavior. I don't think Cameron would have had all the issues he encountered if his dad had not died.

APRIL 2002

My mom, stepdad and sister, Jacque, drove out for a visit. I took them to Fort Worth to visit the Stockyards, which is a great Texan experience. Another day we girls visited the *Dallas* set, Southfork Ranch, located in Parker, TX. That was a fun day remembering that show; I was an avid fan of the show! Cameron made appearances, but he didn't really want to be included in anything other than eating dinner with us.

Our first realization that Cameron was not coping with the death of his father, was one afternoon when we received a phone call from the assistant principal at his school. He reported that Cameron tried to burn his shirt with a lighter on the school bus.

He was in trouble because he had a lighter, not that he was trying to torch himself.

This sent up red flags to me even though I didn't know much about the grieving process for a teenager. My brain clicked in and I knew I had to get him to a therapist. We needed to determine if Cameron was depressed because of his dad's death or something else. I <u>had</u> to take the first step in helping my son.

In hindsight I wish I had read some material on what to do when a child loses a parent or someone close. Instead, I took Cameron to a psychologist. His first appointment with Dr. Rode was May 20th.

MAY 2002

Cameron asked me to drive him to The Wherehouse music store so he could look at CDs. I stayed in the car while he looked around. After 10 minutes, Cameron came out of the store with a manager following him.

> The manager stated, "Your son was trying to steal some CDs."
>
> Cameron declared, "I was not."
>
> I asked the manager, "Did you see anything? Why did you assume he was stealing something?"
>
> The manager responded, "One of my employee saw him unwrapping cases and I found three empty CD cases. It seems he had some type of tool to tear the plastic covering off quickly."
>
> A Lewisville police officer came over to our car and

said, "I'm writing a Trespassing warrant for your son. Can I get his name and address?"

Instead of charging Cameron with theft, the manager filed a trespassing warrant against Cameron. He received a "Criminal Trespass warning", there was no penalty, and he was not required to appear in court.

I was floored that this happened.

While the police officer was writing the warning, I turned to Cameron and asked, "What the heck just happened?"

He said, "I didn't steal anything. I threw the CDs back when I was leaving the store."

"But you were going to steal them?"

I honestly didn't know what to say. Was he going to steal CDs while I was outside sitting in the car waiting for him? Maybe grief had blurred his thinking because that was just stupid.

This was just the start of the battle with law enforcement in Cameron's life.

***

The next sign that things just weren't right with Cameron's emotional outlook was the egg breaking episode.

Cameron and I were in the kitchen one afternoon after he got home from school.

He was in a glum mood and he confided to me and said, "I just want to break something."

"Really?" I looked around but didn't see anything that he could break at the moment.

"I'm sorry but I don't have anything for you to break right now."

"That's okay" and he headed back upstairs.

But the opportunity came up where he could break some eggs.

Cameron was taking photography at school and one of his projects was to photograph eggs in various places and in different lighting.

One Sunday afternoon we made a plan to accomplish his lighting project. We stopped at the grocery store, bought a dozen eggs and headed north towards Denton.

He shot eggs in trunks of trees, me holding up an egg with something unusual in the background, by buildings, etc.

After getting his shoot, he asked, "Can I break the eggs now?"

I didn't see any harm in this and said, "Sure."

My goal was to find an out of the way place where he could commit this "crime". I drove to a parking lot next to an old building.

He then proceeded to slam the eggs, one at a time, into the side of the building.

He felt great satisfaction after lopping those innocent white eggs and watched them break. He actually had a smile on his face afterwards.

During my own grief later, I also felt the urge to break things and so I destroyed an iron after an upsetting phone call. 'Things" can be replaced, people can't.

***

This was the first of several professionals to see Cameron. The first meeting was very closed lipped; Cameron didn't think he had any issues that needed to be solved. I shared the story of his dad's recent death and the lighter on the bus incident with the doctor.

He did request a second visit and at that visit, Cameron was declared fine.

I knew better, but if the kid won't open up, then I suppose there's nothing you can do. I still feel like a good therapist can get a teen to talk. But what do I know? I'm only a parent not a social or miracle worker!

Cameron didn't want to talk about losing his dad. I would offer stories about his dad trying to keep his memory alive but these stories did not seem to affect Cameron one way or the other. He never asked for more details.

I felt like J.C. must have tainted our relationship in Cameron's eyes in some form or fashion, such as blaming me for the breakup of our marriage. If only Cameron had been older when his dad walked out on us, then he would have remembered the torment I went through, trying to keep it all together. Instead, I was made out to be the bad guy.

I loved J.C. and when he walked out on Cameron and I, it hurt me deeply. Cameron was a mere three months old when that happened. The daily problems of taking care of a baby, getting him to daycare, making sure the old car I had kept running, driving 15 miles to a job, and then doing everything in reverse was extremely trying and tiring.

Cameron was the highlight of my life and he made me extremely happy. He had a bright shining face that lit up when something amused him. He was also a risk taker at an early age, such as sticking a key in an electrical outlet (he found the one I had not protected!).

He made me happy in more ways than he'd ever know.

I asked Cameron's closest friend, Everett, to be there for him if Cameron ever wanted to talk about his dad, or perhaps cry, but as far as I could tell, that never happened. Cameron held his emotions inside, bottled up so tight that no one could dig them out.

Before the end of freshman year, his English teacher required everyone to create a "Freshman Notebook". This was Cameron's page about losing his dad:

> There is nothing worse than the death of a family member. That is how I will remember my freshman year the best. Now for the biggest reason why my freshman year sucked. On March 26, 2002 my father died of cancer.
>
> About 7 years ago, my father had cancer in his arm. It was melanoma but they removed it. Then about 5 or 6 years later, he got brain cancer. This was big. This was the year before I moved to Texas. I was always worried about him. Everyday I would wonder how he was doing and wanted to talk to him. He underwent chemotherapy and radiation.

He was constantly fighting the chemicals in his body more that he was the cancer usually. He lost his hair after the radiation. Then for about a year he seemed almost fine like everything was all right. Of course he was tired often, but that's just the way dad always was. So we kept in contact through e-mail. This went on for 2 years after moving to Texas.

Then, one day I got an e-mail from my mom, stepmother, that he had seizures and had had trouble walking. He had recently undergone a spinal tap because there was a trace of cancer in his spine. And apparently the doctors couldn't find any more cancer in him at that time. He was loosing feeling in his leg and soon had to be pushed around in a wheelchair. By the time I knew about this, it was after I arrived home from England. So two days later I flew to North Carolina with my "real" mom. There I stayed with her. Dad was extremely bad off. He couldn't move his arms for an extended period of time, he had t have an oxygen mask and he couldn't talk. That was probably the scariest thing I've ever seen in my life.

Carolyn wanted to take me back home with her because she thought my education was important. Yet somehow she didn't notice the man she had apparently loved for 14 years of her life lying on his death bed. She wanted to take me home, but I simply told her that I wasn't going. She went home and I stayed. Me and Julia, my sister, decided to sleep at the hospital with my mom that night. He died at about 1 in the morning that same night. That night I lost my father, and my best friend. I can't ever get that back. Nothing will ever be the same. And for that, I will always remember my freshman year.

Cameron was never the same happy kid that he was before his dad died.

Note: Cameron went back to the pages in this recollection of his freshman year and drew pictures on the facing pages. Most of the drawings are very dark and depressing.

On the page facing the story about his dad's death, he drew an angel and wrote, "Temptation" with a torn heart below it. Sad.

On the final page of his freshman notebook, he had to write something good about his freshman year – it's blank. On the facing page, he drew a picture of a teddy bear hanging by a rope. He went on to draw this image over and over again in the future.

Cameron's freshman school year came to a close and that summer was different for him since his dad was now gone, but he still wanted to visit Nannette and Jewels (Julia), so I let him. If it brings him comfort to go see them, then I'm good with that.

2002 – 2003
SOPHOMORE

AUGUST 2002

Cameron was back to school having survived his freshman year, as well as his dad's death.

On August 30, Cameron was at school and many students were gathered on the front lawn for some type of event. While the principal was speaking to the crowd, Cameron was talking to his friends and loudly said, "Fuck you."

According to the principal's report, he received an Infraction for "Profanity - Screamed 'fu—' in front of school with 150 people present." He received two days of P.A.S. at school as well as a citation for "Disorderly Conduct" from the school law enforcement officer. This ticket required him to go to court to face a judge. He received a letter from the Court to appear on September 9, 2002 at 9:00 am.

Ugh - another issue but not a warning this time.

> When he shared this information with me, I asked my troubled child, "Cameron what happened that you got a citation?"
>
> He said, "I was with a bunch of people and they kept

bugging me so I say "FU."

I could see how that could happen. He was on edge and grieving.

I then asked him, "Next time, please think before you blurt out bad words. Okay?"

"I'll try."

What would this school year bring for our family? Cameron was certainly depressed even though I didn't know all the signs. Though, he was mostly down and rarely happy.

SEPTEMBER 2002

My friend Karla came out for a short visit from North Carolina. We visited Frisco and the countryside between there and home. We also went to the Dallas World Aquarium. We had fun chatting, eating, and taking pictures. Cameron stayed holed up in his room. However, it was nice having another "girl" to talk to about the issues surrounding Cameron.

On September 19, Cameron went to court for the profanity charge. He pleaded no contest and the fine was set at $252. They suspended payment until March 17, 2003 since he entered a plea no contest, but he did have to pay $52 by October 19.

Cameron must be a good boy for 5 months! He also had to perform 20 hours of community service by January 19, 2003.

I started looking for community service opportunities for my son. It seems as though this usually lands on the parent's lap to manage. It would be nice if the court system handed you a sheet of paper with places that offered community service hours.

2002 - 2003 Sophomore

I contacted the Humane Society of Lewisville and they were happy to have his help. Cameron also helped out the Recreation and Leisure Services Department for the Town of Flower Mound. I think it was for a fishing activity with children.

***

You would think after all that he would never do anything wrong again, but he did.

We told Cameron that he could not go a friend's house one evening, but he went anyway and stayed gone for several hours.

A week later, I was in his room talking to him about his behavior and he said, "I just want to hurt myself."

He then proceeded to take a pair of scissors and scratched his face with them while I was talking to him! I was stunned and frightened at that point. Where would all this lead?

He was already going to a therapist but apparently, that was not working out because he continued to disobey our requests and still showed signs of depression.

I know it seemed like we didn't do enough, but Dan and I both worked full-time and had activities that we enjoyed. We always invited Cameron to join us but as he got older, he refused more and more. That was understandable because we all do that as we start to gain a sense of self during our teen years.

I was not aware of the signs of depression and grief and I wish one of the therapists had educated me on those topics. It seemed Cameron went a long time without any professional trying antidepressants for his depression.

Cameron seemed to do his worst under the radar – at home and at school.

Cameron wrote a paper for English about how much he hated moving to Texas. That was three years ago!

He started out by saying that he'd heard the words, "We're moving" all his life. That was pretty sad. I'm partially to blame but my parents did the same thing to me and I survived. Cameron did not like the idea of moving to Texas but he grew to like the people that he came in contact with.

What he hated the most was the actual move from North Carolina to Texas, via a car show in Kentucky. On top of that, his pet hamster died enroute. At least he took the blame because he said was given the choice to move with us or stay put with his dad. However, I don't remember giving him a choice.

OCTOBER 2002

Since Cameron was on the newspaper staff, he had gotten hooked on photography in a big way. So much so, that Dan let Cameron use his Nikon 35mm camera whenever he wanted.

Cameron had an assignment to shoot some seasonal pictures so we went to a pumpkin patch in Flower Mound. He got many great photos. I have a picture of him sitting on the ground in a pen with goats. I also remembered him taking pictures of children who were there to pick out the perfect plump pumpkin.

His girlfriend, Amy, and her friends started showing up at our house. Not that it was forbidden, just unusual, because normally they liked to do things secretly.

NOVEMBER 2002

Cameron expressed all the signs of someone in deep depression after his dad died in 2001. Yet he never felt comfortable enough to talk to anyone about his depression. He turned to self-medicating which only fueled the depression further.

Signs of depression to watch for:

Overly sullen

Clothing change - sloppier, dirty, not caring how they look

Diet change-

- Eating excessive sweets
- Not caring about what they are eating
- Not eating normally
- Not eating much

School grades change dramatically-

- A usually 'A' student starts bringing home D's and F's
- Not caring if they complete projects
- Always saying they don't have homework – we know better
- Ask their teachers if they have noticed a personality or behavior change

Violent behavior

Wanting to break things

Yelling

Getting into trouble with police while out

Cutting themselves (see section on Cutting)

Lack of communication with family members

DECEMBER 2002

Cameron's grades started to drop. He had earned mostly A's and B's last school year, but it became B's and C's.

We had plans to fly back to North Carolina and Wisconsin for the holidays but before we left, Cameron was gifted with two rabbits. He pretended he didn't know where they came from.

"Cameron – where did the rabbits come from?"

"I dunno. Aren't they cute? Feel how soft it is." while forcing me to rub one of the rabbits.

"Yes, it's very soft but it's not practical for you to have rabbits now when we're getting ready to leave for North Carolina. Plus, I really don't want you to have a rabbit. They require a lot more time and clean up than a small hamster."

"But mom..."

"Nope. Call whoever brought them here and have them take the rabbits to their house. Sorry."

Cameron proceeded to call the culprit and low and behold, Amy showed up the next morning to retrieve her "gift."

***

The next day, we left for our dual city holiday visits to Raleigh and Wisconsin. Cameron was not sociable with most everyone, even around my family, which was out of the norm for him. I wish he had been more social with my nephew and nieces. He didn't want to be in any pictures and he was always turned away when he did end up in a picture.

While in Wisconsin visiting with one of Dan's nieces, Cameron decided to go play with Ryan who was 14 months old. Cameron went into his room, sat on the floor and looked at all the cool toys. Maybe he was missing the simpler days of this past. Cameron used to adore the Teenage Mutant Ninja Turtles. He used to love to sword fight with me every change he got!

Dan did something similar by sitting on the floor in the living room and played with Caitlyn, who was Ryan's big sister by a couple of years. It was sweet seeing these two guys playing with kids and their toys.

JANUARY 2003

Cameron started driver education classes! Yikes! Another driver in the family!

> To kick off the year, Cameron announced to me "I think I'm gay."
>
> I responded, "Why do you think that?"
>
> "Because I like Everett so much."
>
> I share, "Everyone has friends of the same sex and but that doesn't necessarily make you gay."

Yet, also in January while putting away Cameron's clean clothes in his bedroom, I discovered pregnancy information lying around. That surely didn't point to a sexual identity problem to me.

There were also notes sent home from school that never made it to me. I wished the school would have mailed the information because rarely did Cameron willingly share papers he received at school with me.

Cameron was trying to break out of Amy's clutches. He apparently discovered that other girls found him attractive, too.

FEBRUARY 2003

Cameron started getting in driving time with Dan and I. He did drive well, I must admit. I had a Pontiac Grand Prix, which was extremely easy to drive but tempting for a teen since it was supercharged. He just knew that was going to be his car eventually. However, it didn't happen that way because I sold it before he got his license and bought a Toyota Solara.

MARCH 2003

Out of the blue, there was talk of a trip to New York City with the theatre class. Cameron was not in the theatre class, but Amy was.

> I asked him, "Why do you want to go on this trip when you're not part of the theatre group?"
>
> "I like the theatre kids. They're a fun crowd to hang out with."
>
> "Can you get me information about the trip so we can make a decision? You know; like the cost, who's going, where you'll be staying?"
>
> He said, "There's a meeting at the school on Thursday with the theatre teacher and other parents."
>
> "Okay. I'll go to try and learn more. I still think it's strange that you haven't mentioned this until now."

It seemed the reason he reluctantly mentioned it was because Amy wanted him to go and he didn't want to. I think he was trying to break away from her, not spend _more_ time with her. I'm sure he wanted to go to New York though because it was one of those "cool" places to go but he did not necessarily want to go with Amy.

Needless to say, this was not a cheap trip but I felt that Cameron would benefit from seeing a variety of plays as well as visiting New York City.

As a result of hanging out the fun theater kids, Cameron arrives home one day after school with a really odd hair color. He had let Amy bleach his hair while at school.

> "Cameron! What's up with your hair?"
>
> "Amy and some kids from the theatre class wanted to bleach it."
>
> "Well they did a terrible job! It's not easy to bleach dark brown hair. Your hair is orange now. I think you should dye it back to a dark brown."
>
> "Yeah, I guess you're right."

Shortly after that, he did dye his hair but to a very dark brown, almost black shade. Such an experimental kind of guy!

***

A few days went by and I discovered that Cameron was cutting himself, again with scissors. He had cuts on his arms.

> I said, while looking at the red scars on his arms terrified, "What happened to your arms?"

"I cut them." He said matter of factly.

"With what? Why would you do that?"

Cameron states simply, "I was in a bad mood."

I implored him, "Please don't do that. You could hurt yourself badly."

I didn't know what was going on with him besides that, he always seemed depressed.

Cutting, for those unaware, is when someone purposely cuts slashes on their arms or legs with scissors or a knife. They feel they can control this pain if they can't control the pain of a relationship or depression. Watch out for this in a teen you may know. If they are wearing long sleeves in the heat of the summer, they may be hiding something. If you find bloody items in their room, question them. They may be deeply depressed and need your intervention.

***

I got him signed up for the New York trip. He, a group of about 20 kids, parent chaperons, and the theatre teacher, flew to New York. I only knew Amy, none of the other students. Theatre kids are artsy and I knew Cameron loved being around them. He had not connected with a group he felt comfortable with yet, so this group worked at the time. They went to see three plays with "Cabaret" being one of them. He didn't share many details about this trip but I could tell he had a good time in spite of Amy being there.

***

They flew back into DFW on Sunday and I was anxious to hear all about his trip. I headed to the airport to pick him up. We always met in the baggage claim area when he flew back in from a trip.

I found him sitting on the edge of the baggage carrousel with Amy hanging onto him. He was barely coherent. I just thought he was sleepy since he was in New York, the city that doesn't sleep. We got his baggage and headed to the car.

He was speaking gibberish all the way home. I didn't know what was wrong with him. As we got close to home, he said he didn't feel well and asked me to pull over. He then leaned out of the car door and threw up. After we got home, he threw up a couple of more times.

I put Cameron to bed and made an appointment for see him to see our family doctor the next morning. Our doctor could not tell what was wrong with Cameron but prescribed an antinauseous medicine. He recovered quickly after that taking the prescribed meds and his diagnosis was "Gastritis."

***

I found out the next month two important facts:

1) Cameron was throwing up because he had taken a large quantity of Amy's pain meds while on the plane and 2) the reason she had pain meds was because she had had an abortion right before the New York trip.

Both events were very mindboggling! My son had possibly tried to end his life and he might have succeeded if he had more pills or if his body had not protected itself.

And an abortion! I was almost a grandmother.

I knew having the abortion was the best for both of them at their young age but I wish I had been privy to all that had happened. I wish Amy's parents had called to talk the situation over with me, but they probably assumed Cameron would have told me. However, I didn't know anything, so I didn't contact them after the fact. What was the point?

They were probably confused as to why I didn't offer to help in the payment of the abortion. There were lots of details that Cameron didn't share with me. I only found out things when there was shock value for him.

After this possible suicide attempt, Dan and I urged Cameron to break it off with Amy. She was not good for him – in more ways than one. She would call him endlessly and yell at him. Cameron would try not speaking to her but Amy would come back with a vengeance. She would see him in school and accuse him of seeing other girls. A co-dependent relationship had formed.

Amy would threaten to kill herself in order to make Cameron feel badly about breaking up with her. This was not good for him mentally so he would try methods to end his own life. He wanted out but didn't know to gracefully get out of this bad relationship.

Once he took lots of melatonin, which merely made him extremely sleepy. I remember him telling me the story and saying that another mom told him that nothing would happen because melatonin was a natural medication. I couldn't help but laugh at him that time!

Cameron had sleep issues starting that year. The cycle had started of staying up late, gong to school, coming home to nap, then staying up late again.

The relationship issue began Cameron's want to escape

his life. Cutting was another way to stop the pain of his failed relationship with his first girlfriend.

All of these occurrences had me searching for another therapist for my depressed son. I located Dr. Tom Massell, and he was willing to start helping Cameron as well as Dan and I because we were confused about what was going on with Cameron.

Dr. Tom was an easygoing man and I felt sure Cameron would like him. He, at least, helped Dan and me understand some teen intricacies.

Cameron wasn't too fond of him though.

APRIL 2003

During April, there was a huge hailstorm, which damaged many roofs, cars, and trucks left outside. Yep, our roof had to be replaced and Dan's pickup truck got pelted as well.

After that, the beautiful blue bonnets, daffodils, tulips, and a variety of flowers blossomed. Texas truly does have interesting weather.

Cameron skipped school for several days. Three and a half days to be precise. What the heck is going on? Is it Amy problems again? This was his way of avoiding Amy at school. He could have asked us for help but most teens like to handle their own problems in their own way.

Prior to missing days, Amy had showed up just before Cameron's Latin class and started screaming at him about seeing other girls. She then started hitting him. Cameron denied the accusations but he wouldn't fight back.

I learned about this abuse from Cameron's Latin teacher whom he trusted with his secrets. Magistra was a mentor for Cameron.

Since he's been skipping class to escape the wrath of Amy, his report card didn't look too great either. Even in Drawing, he failed his exam with a 50 and received a 68 for an average. He didn't even receive credit for taking this class. This was very disappointing because he loved drawing and was very good at it.

He failed his Latin exam with a 69 and averaged a 75. Another subject he loved. Depression held no bars against my son.

***

On April 14, Cameron came out of his room to chat with me while I was on my computer in the loft. He was wearing a black band t-shirt and had many bracelets on, which he started collecting. He also wore a necklace with various items attached to it. His hair was still short. Interesting how he kept it short all through high school. It was probably one less thing to deal with in the morning when getting ready!

The loft was at the top of the spiral staircase. It was open and overlooked the family and dining room. It was very airy which I loved. There were also two windows, which looked down onto our back yard.

I had my roll top desk there. There was a chair beside my desk, which was rarely used and a couch leftover from our last house opposite my desk. It served as a family meeting area many times.

Cameron sauntered over to the couch and flopped down. He started to spill lots of secrets that he has kept bottled up for a very long time.

"What's up?" I ask.

"Not much." was his response.

"Are you still seeing Amy?"

"Not much. She's been hitting me at school."

"What? When did that happen?"

"She went to my Latin class and started accusing me of seeing other girls. I told her I wasn't but she still started kicking and hitting me."

"Oh no! What happened then?"

"Magistra made her stop and leave. It was kinda embarrassing – Amy screaming at me when the whole class was there to see everything."

"That's good that she took up for you. I wish I knew how to get Amy to leave you alone. Is she why you skipped class for so many days?"

"Yeah, I skipped so I wouldn't have to deal with her."

"That's understandable but you can't keep skipping class. Maybe you could come to me for help or at least your counselor at school. And by the way, I was in your room putting away clean clothes and found some pregnancy information in your room. What was that about?"

"Amy had an abortion."

"When was that?"

"Just before the NY trip. Yeah, I took a bunch of her pain pills on the plane coming home."

"I guess she was just too much for you." I didn't know how to respond to his declaration of taking a bunch of pills.

"I guess."

I was floored by all this information! I don't remember how it ended. He probably went out to smoke a cigarette as bad as I hated that. Now what to do with all this new information?

MAY 2003

I headed to NYC for the National Stationery show with a stop in North Carolina to visit family and a short trip to the beach as well. I stayed a couple of nights with my mom, my sister Kristie, and brother-in-law Kelly at Carolina Beach. One of my mom's sisters, Nancy and her husband, came to visit as well.

It was nice to get away from all the Cameron crap for a bit and I feel bad now that I left Dan to deal with him. That wasn't fair, but Cameron rarely got into trouble when I was gone. He and Dan just didn't talk when I was gone.

When I made it to New York, I checked into an old hotel. I wanted to go to the Stationery Show to see if it was something I wanted to do, in order to sell my greeting cards. It was a huge show and I'm enthralled by its enormity!

I was also able to go to "The David Letterman Show" while there. I emailed saying that I was interested in attending a live show prior to leaving Texas. They called me while I was at the beach and asked some questions that only a true David Letterman fan would have the answers to; I passed the simple test and stood in line the day of the show to get my ticket. Jim Carrey was the guest that night but of course, it was hard to see the stage with all the cameras at the foot of the stage. The studio was freezing just as everyone says it is! It was a fun experience.

I returned home after being gone five days. I was ready to see my boys.

***

Cameron was given his first cell phone, a Nokia phone, of course. We hoped he'd be more proactive about contacting us when he was going to be late or if there was a problem of some sort. This was an early birthday present for him.

He was seeing Dr. Tom on a regular basis but I wasn't sure it was helping Cameron all that much because he was still getting into lots of trouble, which I assumed was connected to his depression.

It's funny how compliant Cameron was when it came to seeing a therapist. He goes and doesn't complain about it but he also didn't share any inner thoughts or concerns he could've been having. The therapist would tell us that Cameron wasn't talking so we didn't pursue it further. He saw each therapist or psychologist for six visits each – that's what insurance would pay for. In retrospect, we should have continued therapy with a person he liked.

MAY 29

Cameron turned 16 and it was the last day of school as well! He invited some friends over and they played video games all night. I made him a strawberry cake because he loved strawberries. I think he got that from me eating so many fresh strawberries when I was pregnant with him. I was actually picking strawberries in a field a couple of weeks before he was born!

2002 - 2003 Sophomore

***

Dan found cigarette butts hidden in the yard. He finally determined that Cameron was stealing cigarettes from his carton of cigarettes. Therefore, on top of everything, Cameron was now also a serious smoker. I had hoped that would not happen but it did.

We were upset about Cameron's lack of care about stealing or smoking. It set off a big fight among the three of us.

> Note: Dan and I both smoked so it was only natural that Cameron wouldn't see anything wrong with the habit. I quit the next year to prove to Cameron that quitting could be done. He didn't care.

On May 31, Cameron left us a handwritten proposal regarding the smoking issue. It reads as follows:

A Proposal

Okay, I have a proposal about the smoking situation. Here are the only things it includes:

I will not smoke again

We don't talk to Cameron about him ever having smoked

I will be calm and not do anything unruly and stupid as long as smoking is not mentioned to me

Check my pockets every time I go for walks of go to a friend's house (leaving from home)

Finally, every time I have to go somewhere, tell me

not to drink or do drugs – it sounds stupid but it shows you care.

This is my proposal. I want the two of you to discuss this tonight and tell me your decision tomorrow. Please don't bother me tonight. I'm just going to stay in my room. I don't fell like discussing it tonight. Okay well talk amongst yourselves.

Sorry for killing trust,
Love,
Cameron

The same night he wrote his proposal, Cameron stayed out all night. There was no call on his new phone to let us know where he was.

JUNE 2003

Cameron was 16 and was successful in getting his driver's license! Cameron and I took a trip together – we went to Toronto! That was also the year of SARS (SARS was a flu epidemic and was reported to be in Canada). I wasn't worried about us catching it but customs at the Toronto airport was being careful. Going through customs always makes me feel like I've done something wrong, when I haven't.

I was attending an IABC (International Association of Business Communicators) conference in Toronto courtesy of Nokia. Cameron had a passport from our trip to London the year before. He really didn't show excitement about the prospect of going to Canada but I really didn't either. Since he was into photography now, he took advantage of the change of scenery to shoot some photos.

Since Toronto was so close to Niagara Falls, I thought it would be fun to drive down and see the ballyhooed falls. We arrived a day before the conference started, rented a car, checked into our downtown Toronto hotel, and then headed south to the falls.

As Cameron had his newly acquired driver's license, he asked if he could drive. I thought about all the driving he'd done in the past 6 months with me along and since he did possess a license now, I said "Yes". I also had the opportunity to provide more driving instructions to him on our one-hour drive to the falls.

The highways were nice and not too busy. While we were out, I noticed Cameron driving right up to the back of a car and then hitting the brakes. I informed him that he could adjust his speed by taking his foot of the gas slightly.

"Ohhh" he said.

Hey – kids don't know these things unless you teach them. He took this driving tip back with him and taught it to his friends!

We made it down to the falls without any problems. We stayed on the Canadian side because that's where we were. We felt like "Nay nay nay, we're in Canada and you're not!" to Americans on the other side. It was fun being in a different country yet still being able to see our country.

There were several things to do but I was trying to conserve my money so we didn't take the Maid in the Mist boat ride. Cameron didn't seem to care one way or the other.

However, we did take a tour that went below and behind the falls. That was pretty cool and we wore rain ponchos to keep from getting wet.

We walked along the edge of the falls afterwards taking photos. Crossing the street, there was a beautiful garden, which I loved. Roses were blooming as well as other flowers. This provided a nice background for some pictures. I have one that Cameron shot of me in the garden.

There were restaurants, quaint hotels, and a horse drawn carriage rides in town - very un-American. We opted to eat lunch at Planet Hollywood as Cameron was all about movies. I have never found meals in Planet Hollywood to be very memorable, but the movie memorabilia was great entertainment for Cameron.

We saw all there was to see of Niagara Falls and headed back up to Toronto. The conference I attended started the next morning.

While I was attending the conference, Cameron would roam around the downtown area taking pictures. He enjoyed taking street scene photos while we were there. One evening we both went out and did a photo shoot together on the streets of Toronto.

One evening we went to see the movie, Finding Nemo. We walked to the theater, which was perhaps four blocks away and when we walked out of the theatre, it was pouring rain! We were drenched when we made it back to the hotel but that was all part of the fun on our trip to Canada.

After we get back home, Cameron flew to North Carolina to stay with his sister and stepmom for a few weeks. This was the norm now; in the summer and during Christmas break he would go back and visit.

JULY 2003

Cameron returned home the first week of July. He had to come back earlier than normal because he had to go to Summer School to re-take History, since he failed during the spring semester. He made a 96 this time!

Cameron displayed strong signs of depression during his sophomore year: cutting, possible overdose, blurting out inappropriate language at school, and smoking. I tried to interject some happiness in his life by taking him on two trips and I feel sure the trips helped him some.

Let's see what happens in the next school year. It doesn't look favorable at this point.

2003 - 2004 JUNIOR YEAR

AUGUST 2003

CAMERON HEADED BACK to school as a Junior this year. He was almost done with high school!

SEPTEMBER 2003

Cameron's second serious girlfriend, Kelly, entered his life this year. Kelly was sweet and a bit shy around me. When Cameron complained about Kelly in his journal or a blog post, it was when she talked incessantly, mostly about things she enjoyed. Sometimes it was about shopping or makeup or hair.

There was jealousy involved when Cameron was exclusive to Kelly. There were too many other girls interested in him as well. That's what happens when a guy is good looking and sociable with everyone!

During the first part of September, I received an update from Cameron's AP English teacher. He had received zeros on two quizzes. She stated that he couldn't afford to get any more. His average for the first quarter was 64.9. I decided to have a chat with Cameron about this.

During dinner one evening, I ask Cameron, "What is the problem in your English class?"

He states, "It's too hard."

"But you were bored in your regular English class and now AP-English is too hard. I think maybe it's a case you just don't want to do the work."

"Maybe."

"You need to do the assignments because you're not getting out of this class. You asked for it so you need to see it through."

"Alright."

That seemed too easy and I knew it was going to be agonizing to get him to do his assignments. You think once your kid gets into high school, they know how to study and pass classes, but sometimes you have to repeat the same procedures as you did in elementary and middle schools. Geez.

OCTOBER 2003

Cameron's AP English teacher reached out to me again. I was concerned about Cameron failing his AP English class. I researched how he was doing in his other classes and he was not doing what he was capable of, that's for sure. His grades were dropping fast. What has happened at school or otherwise that has made him lose focus?

My next discovery might offer an answer to that question.

Earlier in the fall, I noticed Cameron's savings account balance was getting smaller and smaller. He received Social

Security benefits after his dad's death, which went straight into his savings account. It was not a huge amount but enough that he could get in trouble with it. He generally left the money alone or asked me if he could take some out. It was time to explore where the cash is going. I had a feeling it was drugs.

***

Dan and I decided to go to "Cruisin' the Coast," a classic car show we had been eager to attend for a while. We had several car friends attending, so I knew it would be fun to go and hang out them. The show was located in various towns in coastal Mississippi, which made it an interesting car show to attend. We stayed at the Beau Rivage in Biloxi, MS, which was actually a casino. It was one of the few hotels available along the coast since there was flood damage from recent tropical storms. It was comparable to hotels found in Las Vegas.

We left on a Thursday and returned on Sunday.

We arranged for Cameron to stay with a friend, albeit a friend I never heard of. I made the mistake of not talking with the parents, and I'm not sure why I didn't follow through with that. I was probably excited about going on this trip with Dan, so I trusted Cameron to tell me the truth. He was being a good kid during this time and he didn't seem depressed either.

Cameron was 16 at the time and we just weren't comfortable with him staying at home for three days by himself. I called him daily while we were gone and everything seemed to be fine so I didn't worry about him. Cameron was always mature for his age, or more so than his peers.

2003 - 2004 Junior Year

We arrived home on Sunday afternoon to a clean house. Everything seemed okay until we looked a bit closer. Cameron wasn't home at the time.

There was a large trash bag closed up sitting in the guest room downstairs, which was strange enough but after I opened it, some truths needed to come forth. I found several empty beer bottles!

As I was walking into our bedroom I noticed the head on my collectable Wizard of Oz Dorothy doll was turned around backward. These two things made Dan and I check for other items to see what else might be amiss.

Dan discovered his gold ingot that he had for many years, was not in its usual place in his watch box. This was worth quite a bit, as you can imagine.

I looked through my jewelry armoire and found my rings and earrings were still there. I think, whoever was the thief didn't know what a jewelry armoire was so everything remained intact.

We also thought to check the bottles of alcohol that we kept in the kitchen in an out of the way cabinet (not locked though). We knew the trick of mixing water back into bottles that had clear liquor in them. so we did a sniff test and the bottles seemed terribly watered down.

When Cameron got home that night we confronted him about our suspicions.

> I start, "So Cameron, we found lots of things when we got home that looks like you might have had a party here while we were gone. Is that true?"
>
> "Yes. But it was only one night. I spent the other nights at Zach's house. And I had everyone park

down the street so none of the neighbors would be suspicious."

Dan asked Cameron, "You know we can tell that you have replaced some of the clear booze with water, right? It's an old trick. How long have you been drinking?"

Cameron responded, "Yeah, you're right. I've been drinking for the past year."

"And we noticed some other things that weren't right. You forgot a trash bag in the guest room and it had empty beer bottles in it. And the gold ingot in my watch box is missing. Do you know anything about that?"

"There was a girl here who's a crack head. She must have stolen it."

That sounded feasible to me as I had a boyfriend, once upon a time, who smoked crack and things I treasured would disappear as well.

We were upset on many levels but mostly we were sad that the trust that we had placed in Cameron was for naught. Cameron took advantage of our trust in him.

Dan and I never went on any more trips that didn't include Cameron. We either traveled separately or he went with us.

Of course, we had to punish Cameron for his lying about staying at a friend's house and having a party without our permission. He was grounded for a month.

No friends over, straight home after school unless he was

working, no going out on the weekends - the normal grounding rules. Cameron didn't balk because in his mind, it was all worth it.

Dan asked Cameron to write a paper concerning trust since we don't trust him so much any more. He wanted to see what Cameron would discover about trust and a family.

This is what Cameron wrote ...

> Trust
> What it means to members of a family
>
> How other family members should react when one member breaks trust
>
> How trust can be restored after its broken
>
> Trust is said to be the "glue" that holds families together. This is true in most cases. Sometimes it's all about legal ages, emancipation, money, etc. Trust to families is very important. Without trust, what is left to go on? Usually when trust is lost, people stop believing each other, lies start happening more often, and everything just keeps going downhill. That's why most people try to keep trust alive in their homes.
>
> How should family members react? What kind of question is that? It's not a matter of how they **should** react but of how they **will** react. As bad as it

sounds, it happens to everyone. Almost every child breaks the trust of his/her family. The kid could lie, get wasted, total a car, the list goes on. So it's not a matter of how the adult should react, because it's all free-will(sic). Different people will react differently. So...there.

How **can** trust be restored after it's broken? This question...I have no answer to. Thinking for two days got me nowhere...but very quickly. I'm assuming...it has to be built up or some weird crap like that. So the simple answer to this question is: I don't know.

So this essay did not turn to be as long as I had first imagined, but I realized after the second sentence in the first paragraph that this topic... is one heard around the world by millions of families. And I don't know if these three questions were assigned because you really didn't know the answers or if you just wanted my input. Either way, they're answered as best I can...answer them...yeah. So that's all. Questions answered...paper finished...it's all peachy.

He also insets the definition of trust at the bottom. He did this often as he worked through essays. Cameron became a master of the English language.

We later found out from his friends that it was an awesome party. They shared some details with me: his friends all parked down the street from our house so our neighbors wouldn't know what was going on and Cameron kept the noise level down and made sure his friends weren't too crazy outside. It figures that Cameron would throw a great party; he was just that kind of guy.

Later in the month we discovered that Cameron had been smoking in his bedroom.

I had a talk with him in his room.

> "Cameron you know you can't smoke in the house. I don't want you to smoke period."

> While I'm in his room, he shared with me all the evil things he'd been up to.

> "So what? The smoking is nothing! I've been drinking and stealing Triple C so I can take them and sell them."

I'm floored again by this submission. My child smokes, drinks alcohol, skips school, gets a girl pregnant, sneaks out at night – how is this all going to turn out?

NOVEMBER 2003

Cameron emails me an article he found online entitled "A Flapper's Appeal to Parents" which was written in 1922 by Ellen Welles Page. It is very good and would be good for every generation.

The last paragraph stated...

> "... Believe in us, that we may learn to believe in ourselves, in humanity, in God! Be the living examples of your teachings that you may inspire us

with hope and courage, understanding and truth, love and faith. Remember that we are the parents of the future. Help us to be worthy of the sacred trust that will be ours. Make your lives such an inspiration to us that we in our turn will strive to become an inspiration to our children and to the ages! Is that too much to ask?"

On November 23, Cameron was at Everett's house for their usual Friday night of gaming, eating pizza, and assorted junk food (AKA being teens). He looked forward to these nights because Everett was an important friend to him. Cameron admired Everett's drawings from their days together in art classes. Emulating Everett's style of drawing, Cameron became very good at pen and ink drawings himself.

After this one particular night, we received a phone call from Everett around 3:00 p.m.

"Hey, Everett here. Cameron is having seizures. We've called 911 to take him to the ER. You might want to come over."

Dan and I rushed over to Everett's house, as this was not the norm for my son. I had no idea why he'd have a seizure.

By the time we arrived, they were loading Cameron into the emergency vehicle. They asked me if I wanted to ride along and I said, "Yes." Dan drove my car to the hospital in Lewisville.

The EMS report showed that Cameron's respiration was shallow, he was disoriented, and his skin was pale. They gave him Narcan IV, Thiamine IV, and saline.

They checked his blood sugar and did a drug screen. Cameron's blood sugar was fine and his drug screen was clear. Although, he did admit that he took eight tabs of Triple C two days before (probably the night before), which might have had something to do with the seizure.

We were baffled. Upon Cameron's discharge, shortly after we arrived, they told us to make an appointment with a neurologist ASAP to find why the seizure occurred.

I made an appointment with a neurologist, Dr. Solomon, located in Grapevine. He saw Cameron a few days later.

At the appointment, Cameron shared everything that was going on that night in order to shed some light on his condition.

> He said, "We just played video games and I ate a little pizza. I didn't really sleep much."

The doctor summed up the seizure to not enough sleep nor food and strobe light effect from video games. To be safe, he ordered a MRI and EEG to be sure there was nothing else going on inside Cameron's brain. These were scheduled for January.

But the doctor also requested that Cameron not drive for the next month.

> He said, "Having a seizure is serious. We want to be sure you won't have anymore before you drive again. I'd like for you to not drive for a month."

Boy, Cameron was not happy about that.

> "What? I can't drive?"
>
> I say "Nope. It's too dangerous. What if you're

driving your friends around and you have a seizure that results in an accident. I'm sure you don't want that to happen."

His response "No. I guess I can get rides when I need to go somewhere."

He wasn't thrilled but he understood – somewhat.

Telling a teen they can't drive for a month is horrendous to them!

DECEMBER 2003

Having a seizure didn't stop Cameron from continuing his drug experimentation. Hard to believe but it's true.

One evening he came downstairs to the kitchen where Dan and I were talking and it was obvious he was high on something.

I asked him, "Cameron, are you taking something? You don't seem right at all. You know you could overdose on something."

Cameron stated, "Don't worry. I won't go over the line like some of my friends do."

Dan says, "How do you know what's too much?"

"Don't worry. I have it under control." like he was some kind of substance abuse expert.

Turns out he was taking large amounts of Triple C, as it was nicknamed. It was actually Coricidin Cold and Cough medicine. The kids in our area were stealing it and taking large amounts to get high. This became so prevalent, that grocery and drug stores moved it to behind the counter.

***

Later in the month, there had been some vandalism in our neighborhood. Someone had been smashing Christmas lights that were staked in the ground.

Funny how Dan discovered one of his golf clubs thrown behind the bushes in our front yard, we hated to suspect Cameron of vandalism but it sure seems he'd been up to no good.

Dan did a test to see if Cameron had been sneaking out at night after we go to bed and sure enough it was true.

Immediately Dan activated our house alarm, so each night before we go to bed, it was turned on. This is necessary to keep Cameron safe as one neighbor mentioned he'd shoot whoever was out at night causing trouble, and we believed him.

That's when Cameron became a shut in at night – something he hated greatly. However, the vandalism stopped in our neighborhood and I felt he was safe at home now.

***

I took some family self-portraits of the three of us by the Christmas tree before Cameron left for his trip back to North Carolina. We looked pretty darn happy and were all smiling. I suppose the holidays brought out the best in us.

Dan and I stayed home for Christmas while Cameron went back to North Carolina to visit with Nannette and Julia.

I had decided earlier in the year it was time for us to have a family pet and since it couldn't be a cat due to Dan's allergies, then it would be a dog. The engineer in Dan had him researching which type of dog would be best for us. It needed to be easy to train, easy to maintain (groom), and friendly with people. Since I couldn't have a cat, then it needed to be a small dog that might fit in my lap. Not a tiny dog but a smallish one.

We watched the dog shelter videos and went to online websites looking for the perfect match for our family. While Cameron was away over the holidays, we went to look at a couple of different dogs.

We drove to Euless the day after Christmas and met the family that was fostering a cute little dog that was super friendly. We had to decide right then if we wanted to adopt her or not and we decided, yes.

Dan and I were nervous because we rarely make snap decisions. I cuddled her in my arms on the drive home. We stopped at a pet store to buy all the necessities for a dog: collar, leash, dog bowls, food, and something to sleep in.

We changed her rescue name of Gwen to Sheila. We learned that Sheila was a mixed Sheltie who was around 8 months old. She's something else we can focus on besides Cameron's antics and we hoped Sheila would bring some joy to Cameron's life as well.

JANUARY 2004

Second semester of classes and Cameron's grades have dropped even further. He has a 70 in all classes except for History, which he has a 79. The other classes are AP English, BCIS (business computer application), and Latin.

Perhaps his habitual abuse of Triple C has affected his brain, which is drifting over to the classroom, or he just doesn't care.

***

Cameron had the required EEG and MRI done due to the seizures he had in November. He hated the MRI and it made him nervous. His dad had a brain tumor that ultimately ended his struggle with melanoma. Cameron was afraid the MRI would spot a tumor in his brain. Understandable.

> It was an open MRI, which should have been tolerable but Cameron stated, "That sucked. I hated it."
>
> "I understand. I've had one too and it's not fun to stay still for so long and have to listen to that clunking noise."
>
> "Yeah. Let's get outta here."

He also didn't like that he had to take his earrings out.

The test came back fine. The EEG was done in the doctor's office and that was fine as well.

At the return visit to his neurologist, he announced that everything looked normal. Cameron was free to drive again!

On Friday, Cameron skipped school all day and stayed out all night with his current girlfriend, Kelly. I called trying to reach him but he didn't answer.

I had a flight the next morning for a visit with family and friends in North Carolina. I was worried but Cameron had pulled this stunt before and we felt he would show up later. Dan sent me on my way and he promised to keep me posted when Cameron returned home.

That night I'm out with friends for dinner in Raleigh, sitting at the bar waiting for our table when I get a call from Dan.

> He proceeded to tell me, "Hi honey. I hate to tell you but Cameron has been gone all evening. Kelly's aunt suggested I call the police and file a Missing Person report on them, which I did. I don't know where they are at this point."
>
> "What? No one knows where they are? Surely some of their friends know."
>
> "I don't know. I'll let you know when we find out something."
>
> "Okay."

I shared this with my friends and no one seemed to grasp the importance of this information. I was worried and frantic since I was 2,000 miles away and had no idea what my son was up to this time. Had he overdosed somewhere? Had he and Kelly been in a car accident? Was he even alive?

I called Cameron immediately and the call went straight to his voice mailbox.

> "Cameron – please call me or Dan and let us know you're alright. It's hard for me being so far away and not knowing where you are or what you're up to. There's a Missing Person alert out for you guys. The police are looking for both of you. Please go home so we know you're okay. Alright? Love you."

They returned home Saturday night at 8:30 p.m. I got the news from Dan and was so relieved that they were both safe. Thank God, they are okay but how stupid of them.

What should we do about these disappearances of Cameron's?

I talked to Cameron on the phone Sunday for 30 minutes but he didn't express much concern about his actions.

Our phone conversation:

> I asked, "Where did you guys stay?"
>
> "We stayed at a girl's house. Her parents weren't home."
>
> "How did you find out about the police looking for you?"
>
> "We were shooting pool at a place and a friend told us that the cops were looking for us. We decided we needed to go home to avoid the cops."
>
> "Not your brightest move but I'm glad you're safe. Please don't do that again. You have no idea how worried we all were. And I'm here in Raleigh terrified something bad had happened."
>
> Cameron reassures me, "No worries. It's all good."

Unfortunately I got snowed in and couldn't make it back home until Wednesday.

I discovered in one of Cameron's blogs that a couple of days before they made plans to get "60 bucks of 'dro and smoke it."

Apparently, they accomplished their plans. I also found in his phone that he had messaged a friend that I was out of town. Why was the fact that I was out of town pivotal? He did everything else if I was in town or not.

FEBRUARY 2004

I emailed Cameron's counselor and explained some of Cameron's drug abuse issues and wanted to get in touch with his teachers. She was sweet and wrote back a long email making suggestions on how to get Cameron back on track. I wished I could have followed all her recommendations. It was time for me to take action to get Cameron in gear.

I emailed Cameron's teachers to see if he was completing schoolwork and generally doing okay in class. I was informed that Progress reports were sent home recently but Cameron didn't share them with us.

His English teacher had this to say: "Yes, he is a very bright young man – he just doesn't want to do much."

I suspect Cameron was doing more than smoking pot occasionally so I started looking around his room for signs of drug use. I found a knitted cap perched over a light in a strange way. Inside the cap was a broken light bulb that had residue on it. There were also Q-Tips with black residue around the room. I didn't know what the residue was.

I looked around deeper in his room. I found tiny baggies here and there, which meant he's been smoking meth.

I looked in the closet in his bathroom and discovered a Coke can smashed in sideways with holes in it. This must be another way to smoke something illegal.

Parts of the carpet in his room had been loosened around the edges – probably so he can hide drugs there.

He carelessly left lots of empty sheets of Triple C behind his computer monitor in his hutch.

He had cut open seams in a fur decorative pillow that I gave him for Christmas – probably to stash drugs.

It was terrifying all the evidence I uncovered and no one told me about these hiding places; I just started searching very closely. No, I didn't feel bad about "snooping" in my son's room. As parents, we have every right to do that.

***

We discovered that Cameron was smoking cigarettes in the house, <u>again</u>. The alarm system worked to keep him in but since he was now addicted to nicotine, he had to find a way to smoke. Clever Cameron had to come up with another way to smoke when he was locked in the house for the night.

He was smoking in his bathroom, which was easy to discover because he left the ceiling fan on and there were cigarette butts in the toilet. Did he think we wouldn't find this?

His next hiding spot was in the game room storage space. We found lots of cigarette butts and a beer can in there. He swore he didn't like beer!

Dan put an end to this hiding place by changing out the handle to a locking one. The things we had to do to prevent Cameron from doing crazy things.

Cameron wrote Dan and I a long letter on February 14, 2004. It was focused on his smoking cigarettes and his inability to comply with our rules.

He wrote...

> "Cigarettes, or smoke in general, reminds me of Kelly. I'm not exactly sure why it does, but it does.

> The smell, the taste, the thought of it...for some reason reminds me of her. " He goes to explain more about Kelly"...thinking about her "gives" me "pleasure." It's all a process of "pleasing" myself when I'm not around her. So, if it's pleasing to me, then it must also be beneficial. That's why I feel it's beneficial to smoke."

The next long paragraph explained how good he'd been since he had been grounded for his disappearing act in January. He stated...

> "Since I'm on this tangent (writing), I guess that now would be a decent time to apologize for "running away" too. It was brought to my attention a few days ago that the promise not to "run away" expires when I'm 18. I don't know why I didn't know that beforehand. But now that I know this, I suppose I'll go with it. I PROMISE that I won't do what I did again. I will call one of you beforehand to inform you of where I am, where I'll be and tell you what the plans are. Habe bonum diem." (this translated to "Have a good day.")

***

If the month wasn't going bad enough, I got a phone call from his Florida girlfriend's mother who shared lots information from a letter that Cameron had mailed to Erin.

Erin had known Cameron since he was in 8th grade. He met Erin on a trip to Florida with Everett. (Erin lived in upper New

York at the time of Cameron's graduation). They confided in each other over the years and the two of them had a special kind of love. She was a beautiful young woman, well-mannered yet very quiet. She was also quirky, like Cameron.

She said that Cameron was bragging about his exploits with drinking and taking drugs. Erin's mom was worried about what her daughter might be doing as well.

There was also a picture of Cameron with his tongue pierced. When did that happen?

This letter was written the end of January / beginning of February. Guess it took him a long time to explain everything to her.

Erin's mom got off the phone quickly. Perhaps Erin was nearby and she was angry about the phone call.

She called back in a few days and read the entire letter to me.

What an eye opener!

Cameron wrote that he drank Scotch before going to class. He mentioned shooting someone in the foot rather than the face and lots of other crazy, nonsense talk.

I do recall Cameron's breath some mornings and thought it was mouthwash since he had asked for some about a month before. He was setting me up and I didn't even know it.

This was a turning point for me – drinking before going to school? That was serious. Of course, all of his actions were serious but this one woke me up.

My frustration was growing, so I called my Employee Assistance Program to get help from them and they suggested I set up an appointment with a new therapist for Cameron. He quit going to see Dr. Tom because he wasn't getting anything out of those sessions.

I didn't know who else to call, so I resorted to Dr. Tom who understood teens well. I called him out of desperation and asked what we should do. I told him everything that was going on and he suggested The Seay Center at this point. The Seay Center was a drug and alcohol rehabilitation center for teens located in Plano.

MARCH 2004

On March 4, I called The Seay Center and made an appointment for an assessment. His appointment was for March 9. We were given the usual insurance type questionnaire and Cameron was asked to pee in a cup for a drug test.

Cameron was then given a long questionnaire full of questions that he must answer, not just drug related but also criminal activity type questions.

I watched Cameron answer the questions and was astounded by everything he'd been up to!

There were lots of incidents of alcohol and drug abuse which was no surprise but the other stuff – wow!

- Breaking into cars and houses
- Damage to personal property
- Suicidal thoughts
- Addiction to ice (aka meth)
- Drinking before school

The psychologist asked us to come into her office. She looked over everything and said that Cameron definitely needed help.

She felt that the outpatient program, 1-2 weeks, would work for Cameron.

Cameron got upset and stormed out of the office after hearing that he does need help and should go to rehab. I found him outside crying.

> He said, "I don't feel like I have any problems. I can handle it. No! I will not go to rehab!"
>
> "But Cameron you have serious problems. Suicidal thoughts? That's extremely serious. Please go to the Seay Center."
>
> He firmly stated, "No."

Since he's so mad at this point I decided to take him home and talk to him further about our concerns.

I was told as we were leaving that there was space for him there, but we had to let them know in a day or two because they filled up quickly.

Dan and I talked to Cameron over and over that evening about going to rehab and finally he agreed to go. Thank you, God!

I called the next day and got him into a program which took place during his Spring Break.

He would be in an intensive outpatient drug rehabilitation program. I prayed this would help my son finish high school and stop abusing drugs and alcohol.

Cameron went to the Center Monday through Thursday from 3:30 – 6:30 pm. Dan took him and I went to the one-hour parents session at 5:30 and brought him home.

Cameron used drugs the second day at IOP (Intensive

Outpatient Program)! He just didn't get it. They provided a urine drug test at the start of each day he was there. They had to explain to him that he couldn't use ANY drugs. I believe he had taken an Adderal to get through classes that day (spring break had not started yet).

My birthday was on the 16th and Cameron was driving us home. He told me something that I still can't get out of my head and it wasn't drug related.

> Cameron stated, "I'm still mad at you for trying to get me to leave the hospital when Dad was dying."

I was stunned by this as I thought that was in past. I had no idea he was upset about that.

> "Cameron I'm sorry. I had no idea your dad was dying when we were there. I didn't know until that day we were to leave. Three of his doctors cornered me in a room and told me then. I did let you stay, remember?"
>
> "Yeah maybe. I'm also pissed that Dan made us move to Texas and then he lost his job."
>
> "Yeah, none of us were happy about the job loss but we had to move since there no jobs in Raleigh. And Texas has turned out to be a good place for us. You have made lots of friends here."
>
> Cameron stated, "Texas sucks."

What a proclamation – and on my birthday. It sounded like he was expressing anger about his dad's death. Finally.

On Friday that week, Cameron "graduated" from the Seay Center. They felt two weeks was enough, even though I had my doubts. Cameron attended the IOP (Intensive Outpatient Program) at Seay Center for 9 days.

We sat in a large conference room with the parents and their teens. All the teens shared why they were there. There were cutting issues, pot addiction, alcohol addiction, meth addiction, and more. It was almost comforting to see so many other parents there having problems with their teens, too.

Dan and I also meet with Jessica, Cameron's addiction counselor for an evaluation.

> She stated, "Meth is a strong drug to recover from. Don't be surprised if he starts using again in 9 months. Make sure he attends AA or NA meetings weekly. That will help keep him clean."

Some observations about Cameron from his addiction counselor:

> He appears guarded and one senses pain underneath his well-defined presentation.
>
> He has not worked through his grief; he's not trusting.
>
> His brain moves fast so he self-medicates with meth.
>
> Boredom is a trigger.
>
> I need to tell Cameron how I feel.

His discharge diagnosis: Alcohol abuse; cannabis abuse; major depressive disorder, single: Hx of amphetamine abuse, Hx of OTC medicines.

2003 - 2004 Junior Year

> Some highlights at his discharge: Cameron is stable at discharge, denying suicidality, homcoidalit, and no evidence of a thought disorder. Cameron is attending AA meeting regularly but has not obtained a sponsor. Cameron minimizes his drug and alcohol problem, and continues to state that he can and will stay clean and sober without a recovery program. He denies feeling depressed currently and his presentation is generally stable and aloof, but engaging when addressed. Cameron is an intelligent young person who appears guarded and one senses that there is pain underneath his well-defined presentation. If Cameron is able to allow a therapeutic alliance to develop with an outpatient therapist, he has the capacity to work through issues that may allow him to develop deeper relationships with others, including himself.

After the parents meetings, which helped us learn how to deal with our teen, I was ready and anxious to keep Cameron clean! I witnessed how great Cameron looked and appeared to feel after he stopped abusing drugs; I wanted that to continue. It wouldn't be easy for him or us, but his life and wellbeing was worth the effort!

Our son was clean! Free of his addictions – for now.

I found where AA meetings were held in downtown Lewisville. I went with him to a couple and then sent him on his own to attend after that. One of his friends attended groups as well, so sometimes they went together.

That didn't last too long. It's hard for adults to attend every week much less a teenager who may think they have far better things to do than listen to adult alcoholics. There was one for teens but it was in Grapevine, which was a distance to drive.

Yeah, I should have driven him to the one in Grapevine but I had things in my life going on as well.

We also located a new psychologist for Cameron, Dr. Talon, located in Highland Village. It was recommended by The Seay Center that he continue seeing a therapist. However, Dr. Talon was getting the silent treatment from him, so I stop taking him to her before the usual six-week limit. Teens are funny about who they will share with. If it's not working, then it's best to find another one they will talk with.

Cameron first anti-depressant was prescribed to him from our family doctor: Wellbutrin 150 mg 2x day. I don't remember but perhaps Dr. Talon recommended it.

***

I flew to Atlanta for a Nokia event for three nights. My sister, Kristie, came down to visit with me for a couple of days while I was there. It was so great to be with her and talk about the Cameron issues.

Later in the month, Cameron was tired of being grounded all the time, so Dan made a deal with him: get a job and you won't be grounded. Cameron was at the six-week mark for being grounded for an assortment of reasons.

We also implemented, "Cameron's House Rules", which was recommended by The Seay Center. They were as follows:

Rules not to be broken:

No skipping classes or whole days of school

No sneaking out of the house

No selling or using drugs or alcohol

No physical violence towards others

No self mutilation or suicidal attempts

No smoking in the house

Attempt to quit smoking by 9/01/04

Rules that can be discussed upon Special Request:

Music off during sleeping hours to ensure good sleep patterns

To bed by 11:00 p.m. Sun – Thursday

When leaving the house, we must know the following:

People you'll be with

Location

Verifiable information

When we call your mobile – you must answer or call back within the hour

Curfew on schools night/others: 10:00 p.m.

Curfew on weekends: 11:00 p.m.

In order to spend the night at a friend's house, we will need the following:

Name

Address/phone number of house

Verification from parent

Homework to be done nightly (and completely)

Chores:

Empty dishwasher when clean

Remove trash from upstairs on Monday nights

Dirty clothes downstairs by 8:00 a.m. Sundays

Bathroom to be cleaned on the 1st Saturday by 6 p.m. every month

Your room is to be kept tidy. Room to be vacuumed, dusted, picked up 2nd and 4th Saturday by 6 p.m. every month.

Above and Beyond:

Cook dinner for family

Reward?

Wash car with soap, sponge, water, and then dry with cloth

Reward?

Mow grass

Reward?

Edge grass: sidewalks, around house and fences

Reward?

Agreed upon by:

_____   _____   _____

Date: _____

This looks somewhat childish or barbaric but it worked – for a while. It was helpful to have everything down on paper. As an adult you already know most of these, they are common sense rules - but teens and younger, need to have rules in writing if you want them followed.

APRIL 2004

Prom month. Since Cameron and Kelly were both grounded for being MIA in March we had to make a difficult decision; should we let them go to prom? We, the parents and guardians, decided to let them go since the tickets were already bought and maybe some happiness would improve the situation.

Cameron was excited about renting a tux for the prom! We found a burgundy one, which looked great on him and he wore his "Chucks" sneakers with it.

Kelly had a burgundy dress and she wore her Chucks as well. They looked great together. I took pictures but didn't use a flash, so the pictures weren't that good. I hate that!

Kelly's aunt and uncle, who she and her sister lived with, drove them to the Dallas hotel where the prom was held. However, they didn't get to party afterwards as many teens do in Texas. Cameron had a good time with his friends but he said he wouldn't go to another prom.

***

One of Cameron's friends told me that Cameron was not taking his anti-depressants, because it made him feel like a zombie. Some anti-depressants do that. I took Cameron back to the doctor to switch meds and he was put on Lexapro.

April 16, 2004 – Cameron got a speeding ticket for driving 42 mph in a 25 mph speed zone. He got it excused by taking a driver's safety course.

Dan went to Oklahoma City for the weekend for a car show. I knew he needed a break from us, so I stayed home with Cameron. It's good for everyone to get breaks from the crap that goes on at home but it has eased up tremendously since Cameron was drug-free at the time.

MAY 2004

This month, Dan and I found pot in Cameron's bathroom, which resulted in a big blow out between the three of us. Cameron said he's tired of being grounded so he turned to drugs again.

He called Dan lots of names – it was not a pretty situation.

The argument ended up in our master bathroom. Cameron was sitting on the edge of the garden tub and Dan was leaning against the vanities. I found them in there and sat on the edge of our bed; the door to the bathroom opened up right there.

As they weren't getting anywhere in their argument, I pulled the "dad" card.

> "Cameron, I feel sure your dad would not approve of your drug use."

Cameron glared at me and started crying.

He got up and stormed into the kitchen and pulled out a large knife from the wooden knife block that sat on the long counter.

"Cameron! What are you going to do with that?" He was scaring me terribly!

He threw it down on the counter and says "Never mind. It wouldn't help anyway."

I didn't understand what his intent was. Was he going to use it on himself, Dan, who?

He then headed upstairs to his room. We all needed to calm down after that point.

This fight upset Dan so much that he stopped talking to me for a couple of days. He finally broke his silence and told me that if there's another fight like the last one either he goes or Cameron goes. It was a terrifying fight.

Dan went in to talk to Dr. Talon about Cameron. He seemed more understanding of Cameron after talking with her.

Cameron was failing algebra due to sleeping in class. Yet, before the end of the school year, he took the TAKS test and exceeded the standard level on all areas. TAKS is the Texas Assessment of Knowledge and Skills test given to students. He achieved "commended performances" in Social Studies.

According to his report card though, he barely passed AP English, Latin, and US History. Therefore, we knew he was smart but he definitely did not want to apply himself in classes. I wonder now if an online class would have been the answer for my son.

***

Cameron wrote a blog after downing lots of vodka at a party with a girl in our neighborhood; he was a bit tipsy (or perhaps very drunk). Mind you this is just a few months after rehab.

In the blog he said that "The Breakfast Club" was one of his favorite movies and he had a "thing" for Molly Ringwald. (He also really likes Drew Barrymore).

> He also said "Kelly and I ARE getting married, ARE having kids, and WILL die loving each other. She's the only things(Sic) that makes me freakishly happy."

I didn't realize he was that much in love with her! Maybe it was the alcohol talking.

Kelly and Cameron started dating when he was a Junior and she a Sophomore. I'm not sure where or how they met, as Cameron was mostly quiet about his relationships until they got out of hand.

Kelly was a quiet girl but she had Cameron's heart, not all the other girls at Marcus who vied for his attention. There were two girls in Cameron's first Latin class that came over to our house occasionally. One was a bit possessive and Cameron said, "She acts like she my mother. I already have a mother."

Kelly and her sister, whose nickname was Chicken, lived close by. Not in our neighborhood but a walkable distance. She seemed to enjoy partying as much as Cameron did though, since they often got into trouble together. I didn't have any issues with her until much later.

2003 - 2004 Junior Year

***

Dan was fed up with Cameron's antics and he threatened to leave if there were more problems. Great – I had two guys in the house mad now.

On Mother's Day Cameron gave me an ugly lamp. It was so strange that I returned it. I was taken to dinner at Pappadeux, which was our favorite restaurant.

I decided a few months earlier to have an exhibit booth at the Stationary Show in New York in hopes of selling my greeting cards, CZ Cards. There were no problems between the boys while I was gone that time but they probably weren't speaking to each other.

I had hoped my greeting card business would take off, so I needed to get out there and show them off. Greeting cards is a hard business to break into.

I was gone for 5 nights. My friend, Karla, from North Carolina met me in New York so I had someone to help me with my booth at the show. We ate at various restaurants and went to a Broadway play in the evenings. We talked to greeting card customers during the day. It was quite an experience. I still don't enjoy New York like so many other people do. It's too noisy and crowded for my taste.

***

After getting back from my trip, Cameron had a minor accident in my car. He rolled into an SUV at a stoplight in Lewisville on his way back to school from Dale Jackson. There wasn't much damage but it still needed to be fixed since my car was pretty new, and since there was no police involvement, there was no ticket – yea!

However, this caused yet another fight between Dan and Cameron. Cameron was mad, he left the house and didn't return that night. Turns out he spent the night in a park by his friend Everett's house.

My, what fun we had together, I think sarcastically.

Cameron turned 17 on May 29. I gifted him a couple of movies he wanted, some undies and a box of lemon bars. Things were still tense at home, so he hung out with Kelly and friends later that day.

Dan only talked bad about Cameron at that time; it wore me down.

JUNE 2004

I wanted to try to have a better month. Dan and I celebrated our seventh wedding anniversary on June 7. We invited Cameron to join us to dinner and he agreed. Yay!

Cameron got his SAT scores back: Math 520 and Verbal 560 for a total of 1080. He wanted to retake it in December to see if he can improve his scores.

He went to court for one of his smoking tickets. Yeah, I know it's silly that he even got a ticket for smoking, but Flower Mound is a small town and it happens.

Cameron made a declaration that he thought he was bisexual. This time it started with a flirtation he had with a guy named Kelly, while his girlfriend Kelly was on vacation.

I believe they only saw each other a few times, but that was enough to confuse Cameron.

Kelly took Cameron to the art museum in Fort Worth one afternoon. Another day I saw him at our house briefly. Cameron seemed taken away with him.

In his blog, he talked about missing his girlfriend, Kelly, and the other Kelly. He also talked about how he needed his "good" friends to keep him off drugs, and he shared much about his encounter with the latest Kelly.

Kelly, the girlfriend, found about the other Kelly. I knew that would prove disastrous! I didn't like the guy Kelly; he was too sneaky acting. Fortunately, Cameron dropped that friendship.

When his friends were out of town, Cameron went to theaters with me to do trailer checks on the weekends. I kind of liked it when his friends are away; that way I could get some time with him!

***

Cameron's dog, Jake, who lived in North Carolina with J.C., died. He was 11 years old. Cameron showed some sadness in a blog but he didn't share much about it to us. He just stepped out his room that afternoon and said, "Jake died."

JULY 2004

Cameron attended the Gloria Shields workshop that his newspaper teacher recommended he attend. It was a newspaper/photography workshop for students to improve their photography, yearbook, and newspaper skills. It was held in Dallas, which meant he got to be away from home for 4 days with likeminded students!

I loved this for him because he was in his element. I liked for him to see that he could have fun and do interesting things while also being mindful of his actions.

***

Shortly after Cameron got back, Dan went to California for a week for work. That left Cameron and I alone.

Cameron blogged about this:

> "My stepdad was out of town in California all week thus far. He came back last night. But I get along so much better with my mother when he's gone. Funny how that happens…So this whole week was amazing…and easy-going. Now that he's back, I can feel the tension building up already. It just happens that way…like black magic I guess.
>
> But, I haven't really been up to anything this week. That was my plan. If I could show how good of a kid I am when he's out of town and still have everything in one piece when my mother got home from work, it would show my "responsibility." Responsibility and trust have nothing to do with it really. I just want them to take things easier. It's not even for MY own good. They just need to sit back and chill…something they've apparently forgotten how to do since they were drowned in this corporate American industry they've been in for a few years. I don't know what it does to people, but apparently it's not pretty. Ever

since I've known Dan, he's been a little uptight...not completely, but a little bit. And ever since my mom started working with Nokia, she's become a bit edgy. She can't take as much "nonsense" as she used to. And it just bugs me. I just wanna sit down with her one day and roll a joint for just her and I to enjoy. Just to see her lighten the f*ck up. (I censor myself to be polite). I know she'd enjoy it if she did it. She used to be a pothead, so I don't see what new leaf I'd be turning for her. Whateva..."

He then headed to North Carolina for three weeks to visit his sister and stepmom. Once there, he complained in another blog that it was too slow there and he missed his friends and girlfriend. There was no pleasing this kid!

Dan admitted to me while Cameron was gone that he didn't like him anymore. That was very upsetting to hear since I loved both of them so much. I didn't want to lose either one of them.

AUGUST 2004

I went to Louisville, KY for a week to sell my CZ Car Cards at a national car show. My mom and stepdad drove from North Carolina to visit with me and to oogle over all the classic cars. This was the same show that Dan, Cameron and I visited on our move to Texas. I was somewhat lonely there by myself as there's not much to do in Louisville unless you're into horses.

Summer was nearing an end but we had two months of miserable heat to contend with.

Cameron headed back to school as a senior!

2004 - 2005
SENIOR YEAR

AUGUST 2004

CAMERON STARTED HIS last year of high school on August 12. I knew he was glad to see all his friends, who he didn't get to see over the summer. Yet, his friends who already graduated, such as Everett, were no longer there so that was probably a disappointment.

Reading Cameron's blogs from this period showed a very dedicated and responsible individual. He was still clean – off alcohol and drugs. His focus was being lead photographer for the school newspaper, "The Marquee." He accepted many challenges for getting photo shoots for the paper. This was his last year and semester to be involved with the paper, a future disappointment.

I loved that he had this newfound focus, but could he maintain it? High school was hard for even the most focused student. Drama always seemed to kick in and disturb everything set in motion already. He started off with seeing Kelly exclusively and ended up the school year with Lauren, which didn't go over well with Kelly.

Cameron has a unique look about him this year. He was no longer chubby like he was in 8th grade. He had grown to 6 feet tall and it was easy to see why the girls wanted to be called "Cameron's girlfriend". I know I'm his mom but damn it, my son was handsome!

His hair was cut rather short and it was dark brown. Sometimes he would try to dye it, which was a mistake, but he tried anyway, or else one of the girls would talk him into it. I tried to tell him it's hard to dye brown hair. If he were here today, no doubt he would try out all the colors that are available – purple, blue – anything outrageous.

He liked to cut his own hair. It was between 2 and 3 inches long and somewhat curly on the top. He doesn't use any hair products; he's just not that kind of guy. I would shave his neck with electric cutters, so at least that area looked nice. We just had that ritual; he'd cut the top and I'll clip the back.

Unfortunately, since he did cut his own hair, sometimes it came out looking terrible! One time one side near his neck and ear was cut really short. I joked with him that he looked like a mental institute patient right out of *One Flew Over the Cuckoo's Nest*.

He also had his own style of dress now. It takes time to work out your own style in high school. You go in looking like everyone else, but slowly you find "yourself".

Cameron generally always wore jeans and either a band T-shirt or dress shirt with a tie. That was his trademark – the tie. He was a unique dresser.

After using meth, he lost enough weight to get into girls junior sized jeans. Yes – female juniors. These were skin tight on him. It seemed he was ahead of his time with clothing. The fad for straight leg tight jeans for men started in 2001. Cameron was on the cusp of its popularity.

He really enjoyed wearing men's dress shirts, not tucked in, with a tie hanging long not pulled tight. White shirts were a favorite but the necks would get really dirty. A favorite tie of his was a blue and green stripe one, as well as a pink one.

Per one of Cameron's blogs...

> "I think I'll dress up today...bust out some tie action. Maybe even the pink tie. Perhaps it would be easier with the classic stock market tie... or even, ol' green-n-blue....checkers, too. I have the necessary ties to survive! In America!"

His Aunt Kristie gave him some cool ones and he enjoyed wearing those as well. One had a chicken with eggs on it. I would venture to say that, Kristie was his favorite aunt since they were both creative types.

Of course, like every other teen, Cameron liked to declare his love for music by wearing his favorite band T-shirts. He wore these mostly when the weather was warmer.

SEPTEMBER 2004

Cameron had a driver's license but as he didn't have a real reason to have his own car, I let him borrow mine from time to time. Since Cameron had been using my car, I found dents and scratches in it. There were scratches from his belt, which had metal studs on it. He would probably lean against the car chatting with someone and scratch the door with his belt. I'm not sure why there was a dent on my roof but he blamed it on Kelly. Teens – they just don't have respect for other people's personal property. So, no more sharing my car unless it's job related, especially because my car was new.

He succeeded in getting his first job at Arby's in Flower Mound. He wasn't thrilled about his first job, but it did get him out of the house and this was important since he was grounded for so long. Of course, he abused this privilege pretty early on. He'd say he was going to work but he wasn't.

Since Cameron was able to get a job, Dan started the hunt for a car for his stepson. After Dan did research on the best type of car to get a teen, he decided that a Taurus would be the safest car for Cameron.

Dan helped Cameron get his first car, a 1993 Taurus, white with a burgundy interior. He was 17 at the time, so I was in total agreement that he get a car. He had money in his savings account from Social Security so that paid for a large portion of the cost and Dan paid for the balance. Also, part of the agreement was that Cameron pay for his own car insurance.

Dan and I went to a car show in Fort Worth on a Sunday, and afterwards we drove out to West Fort Worth to look at a Taurus for Cameron. It wasn't the prettiest car but functional and that was all that was required as a teenager's first car.

Cameron writes in his blog...

> "I'm getting a car tomorrow. I suppose that's another up. Finally, I won't be hitching rides with others...I'll be more free. Took long enough. Whateva..it appears to be a decent car. I don't care what it looks

like. But's white on the outside and burgundy on the inside...ultra-pimpin'. So by afternoon tomorrow, I'll be pimpin' it up...or something."

Cameron also had a lot of photo shoots to accomplish for the school newspaper, so having a car was vital. He also had the job at Arby's so Dan and I felt good about the car purchase.

Cameron really loved his car. He named it Delilah. I remember the feeling when I got my first car. It truly is love. A car equals freedom. If you're feeling down about something, a drive in your car will lift your spirits. If you really want to see your friends, then a car can provide that as well.

Cameron went back to court for his second and third smoking violations. He just didn't care if he was caught. The judge had him perform community service and that was okay with Cameron. This time he helped out with a pet adoption, nonprofit mostly. Texas Tailwaggers invited him to their adoption events and he'd walk the dogs so they could relieve themselves. I went with him once to help out. Stacey and Deb, from Texas Tailwaggers, came to love Cameron, as he was a sweet, caring kid.

Another opportunity presented itself, there was an event in downtown Lewisville called, Lewisville Western Days and since Cameron needed community service hours, I had him call to see if he could help out as a "roadie" with the sound guys and they said, "Yes".

Cameron loved doing this and I encouraged him to seek out similar opportunities.

Lewisville is a sizable town of around 90,000 people but the downtown area was nothing special. I only remember going there for AA meetings with Cameron and taking pictures around Christmas with its town hall decorated in lots of white lights. There was also a huge motorcycle rally in December, where the bikers collected toys for kids so that was a great photo op as well.

The Lewisville Western Days sounded fun but the downtown area didn't really look "western". I stayed and participated in another activity while Cameron was helping the sound guys.

I also discovered how awesome Kettle Popcorn is; Western Days was where I bought my first bag and I've been hooked ever since! The salty popcorn mixed with sugar is a German tradition. Texas has a huge German influence as many settled there during the 1830s.

***

One evening Cameron came home stoned out of his mind. He acted very nonchalant and silly. He had been out with Amy and her friends. Mind you, he was no longer seeing her, supposedly. Apparently, they had been smoking pot.

Dan, Cameron and I went to Dale Jackson Career Center's Open House. Cameron's teacher, Mrs. Harmon, raved about how great a photographer Cameron was! A parent loves to hear positive comments about their child. It was a good evening for all of us. I only wish we had more of those.

The next day we got Cameron's progress reports: F in Economics, yet an A in Advanced Design, which was his class at Dale Jackson. That figures.

The Dale Jackson Career Center was part of the school district. Students could go there for a variety of skill type classes and it was where Cameron learned Graphic Arts. He was quite an accomplished graphic design artist. He was able to blend photography and graphic arts to create advertisements. It also allowed his to utilize his writing talents. He even gathered a lot of support from his teacher.

It was at Dale Jackson where Cameron met Lauren. She resembled Kelly as they both had dark red hair and green eyes. I suppose Cameron was attracted to that combination.

Lauren was not as down to earth as Kelly. She was a poet and more of a free spirit. I recall a conversation I had with Cameron one day while we were in my car after a therapist's appointment.

> He said, "Lauren was talking about being in a canoe. I wish she'd float down the stream in the canoe!"
>
> "What was that about?"
>
> "I have no idea. She says random stuff like that all the time."

He seemed to be angry with her for some unknown reason, although, he didn't share why he was angry.

Lauren lived in Flower Mound as well. She was a year younger than Cameron and had her hopes up that Cameron would take her to the prom when it was her time to go. However, he balked and said he'd never go again.

In Cameron's writings, he referred to Lauren as his "muse." He considered her as a potential life partner since she had different qualities from Kelly. Cameron loved two girls at the same time during this senior year. This was not good.

2004 - 2005 Senior Year

***

Cameron "celebrated" spending one year with Kelly. He's not too enthused by this but maybe he was meeting so many other girls that staying with just Kelly just wasn't fun anymore.

Cameron decided to stop eating.

> Per Cameron..."I like the way it feels when my stomach is empty. And the random "crunch" noise it makes."

This must be another reason he lost so much weight but he doesn't keep this up long. Mind you, he still drank soft drinks like water so he hasn't given up sugar.

Five days after getting the car, Cameron had a minor accident. He was driving back to school from Dale Jackson Career Center, which was about a 10-minute drive, with Lauren after their design class earlier that afternoon.

Along with the accident, he got a ticket for unsafely changing lanes. He had to go to court in January for this ticket.

The accident was minor but it brought up questions about drinking because one of the assistant principals accused them of drinking. I saw Cameron after the accident and I don't recall alcohol on his breath but I learned that Lauren had run into trouble with drinking so that seemed to be following her. At any rate, it was another ticket for Cameron (for us) to deal with.

Cameron received two awards from Marcus that I didn't discover until much later. One was a "Certificate of Achievement for Best Photo" dated September 24, 2004 signed by his Newspaper teacher, Lori Herbst. The second was a "Principal's Award for Outstanding Photographer"!

I wish I knew which photo or photos these awards were for, but this proves that Cameron had low self-esteem, as he never mentioned this to Dan or me. I know I would have been ecstatic about his dedication and achievement and the chance to celebrate something positive with Cameron.

SENIOR PORTRAIT TIME

I took off early from work one afternoon and went with Cameron for his senior pictures appointment. He asked me to go with him, not sure why. I helped him with his clothes, merely by handing him what the next shot required.

Cameron really enjoyed being on the other side of the camera lens. He posed in several settings and showed a variety of facial expressions.

One setting looked like the side of building with artificial grapes draped around. This was one setting he liked the best or at least where the best pictures were taken. I know sometimes when you're having photos taken, the ones near the end are not the best because you're tired of posing and I think this was the case for him as well.

Another was black with a staircase. Nice lighting for this setting but not the best photos. The photographer, fortunately, was game for whatever Cameron and I came up with!

In the casual poses, he seemed deep in thought. Then the graduation gown pictures, he was cutting up. Funny photos!

The pictures of Cameron in the mock tux shirt reminded me of my cousin, Charles. I am so grateful for these posed pictures because there weren't many other great photos of him.

When the proofs came back several weeks later, we had a

really hard time picking the ones we wanted to buy. I bought a lot of prints in various sizes and am glad of it to this day, especially in light of what happened in the future.

Later in the month, I left for Arizona for three days for another IABC conference. It was nice to get away from the craziness at home and I got some beautiful shots of the Sonora Desert while on a Hummer Tour.

All was quiet at home while I was gone.

OCTOBER 2004

Cameron pulled another all-nighter. This time it was after a full day of photo shoot assignments. He was in Dallas, Fort Worth, and Grapevine; that's a lot of miles to cover. I was angry when I learned of all the places he had been because gas was not cheap. This was for the school newspaper and they didn't reimburse students for the money spent while on assignments. (I later found out from the yearbook/newspaper teacher that Cameron had chosen to do all these shoots).

Cameron's car was parked in the driveway when we got up the next morning. He came downstairs to the kitchen where Dan and I were having our coffee (for Dan) and tea (for me).

Dan asked, "Cameron, what happened last night? We saw you weren't home when we went to bed."

Cameron explained it this way, "I was so happy after my shoot, that I stopped in a convenience store, stole three tall boys, drank them fast in the bathroom, then went to my car. I was too drunk to drive so I slept in my car in the parking lot. I drove home at 3:30."

"So do you think you might have a problem? That's not good to drink that much in such a short period of time." said Dan.

"Yeah, I guess I do have a problem," admits Cameron.

I felt happy for him about the photo shoot because he was elated about it, but he made poor decisions on many other accounts. Stealing beer was bad, drinking them all at one time was terrible, then sleeping in your car?!?

He waited until he sobered up before he drove, but we all know that he wasn't really sober. He probably was at a nearby convenience store, which means he didn't have far to drive at least.

For this stunt, he was grounded for two months as well as for past issues. We actually started losing track of what he was being grounded for.

Cameron didn't work at all one week. So I asked him why.

"Cameron, I've noticed you haven't gone to work all week. What's up with that?"

He shrugged and finally said, "The manager didn't like the shoes I wore to work."

"Well, let's go get some Arby's approved shoes then. And after that, I want you to beg to get your job back."

"Alright." He said not enthused at all by this.

He didn't like his job at Arby's. I'm sure he'd preferred to be a famous photographer but we all have to pay our dues.

After we took a quick trip to get some nonskid black shoes, he went in to see the manager.

He showed his manager his new shoes and the manager reluctantly gave him his job back.

***

In order to keep our sanity, Dan and I stayed active with Top Tin, the street rod car club we belonged to. Their annual event, the Goat Roast Car Show, was coming up and I volunteered to plan the route this year. I enlisted Cameron to help me.

We drove from our house in Flower Mound, winding north through the Texas countryside to end up in Muenster where the Goat Roast is held each year (the same car show that Cameron took Amy to a couple of years earlier).

While we were together for a couple of hours, we talked about plans for college.

> I started, "So you think you'll be ready to go to college after graduation?"
>
> "Yeah, I guess so."
>
> "Any idea where you want to go?"
>
> "UNT would be awesome. But I'm not sure they'll accept me."
>
> "We just have to wait and see. I'd love to see you go there, too. They have some great programs. You could learn to become a better photographer. Or maybe graphic design artist."
>
> "True that!"

We had taken a tour of the UNT campus earlier in the year and we both thought it would be a great college for him. He was receiving college information from all types of colleges – mostly design schools.

I loved our alone time together. Cameron would open up to me so much more during those times. Taking off for a trip together was always a pleasure for me. I remember our trip to Canada and to the mountains in North Carolina, when he was eight. I often wished I had not let Cameron go to live with his dad, so we'd have more time together but I felt it was important for him to get to know his father. At that time, I was attending college full time so that was a better option for Cameron.

***

Cameron decided to take lots of Triple C one night.

> I knocked on his door, "Cameron – come downstairs. Dinner's ready."
>
> He responded with a slur, "That's okay. I'll pass tonight."

I opened his door and he's obviously out of it. I saw empty sheets of Triple C lying on the floor. That really pissed me off since we talked about doing drugs over and over. No more drugs in the house. Period!

I threatened to kick him out of the house if he continued to bring in drugs. He shared with me that he was breaking up with Kelly. I guess that seemed like a good enough excuse to abuse drugs, at least in his mind.

He didn't explain why he was breaking up with Kelly but I had my suspicions. Cameron had been seeing a lot of Lauren those days and Kelly may have found out so rather than listening to her, he wanted to break it off. Keep in mind, Cameron was not good at breaking up with girls.

***

One afternoon, when Cameron was driving to Kelly's house he decided to take a short cut and drove over the corner of someone's yard. The owner saw this and found Cameron in his car at Kelly's house, just up the street. The man was very angry and wanted Cameron to get out of the car. Cameron said "No." The man attempts to take Cameron's keys (this is per Cameron's blog post). Naturally Cameron's not going to let that happen, nor would I!

The man threatened to call the police and report the incident. Cameron apologized to the man several times but to no avail. He wanted Cameron to repair the 5-inch ditch in his yard. Cameron said he drove five mph, so he knew there were no ditches left behind.

Cameron came home after seeing Kelly and found a note that he needed to call a police officer regarding the yard incident. He called and told his story to the officer. The officer asked if he could come by and talk to him and Cameron asked that it be soon because he had a photo shoot he needed to do that evening. However, the officer never showed and Cameron missed his deadline.

I suppose he never drove over anyone else's yard after that ordeal. There's some crazy thinking that goes on inside a teen's head!

***

Cameron's senior picture proofs came back. They were <u>fantastic</u>. So many faces of Cameron - serious, funny, confused. He loved posing for the photographer.

I ordered lots of Cameron's senior portraits. It was hard to select because there were so many great ones but I spent $301 on them and now I am so glad that I did!

***

Meanwhile, I was having issues at work (Nokia Mobile Phones), personnel problems. If the home issues weren't enough, now I have work issues, too.

Cameron lied about going to work one night and went to Everett's house instead but he was still grounded for the previous late night excursion.

So that was twice in one week he had not done the right thing. He just seemed to stay in trouble.

NOVEMBER 2004

Cameron was lying about when he was scheduled to work so he wouldn't have to go home to being grounded. He was told to leave work one day due to having nail polish on. Yep, Cameron was unique.

On his way home, he stopped at a car wreck and proceeded to take pictures, thus provoking the police.

He did leave but he also shared this information with us:

"There was the coolest wreck on the way home on 2499! I stopped to take pictures but a cop told me to leave."

I asked, "Why were you told to leave? And why were you even taking pictures of a wreck?"

"The lady who was in the wreck asked me to stop taking pictures. So the cop asked me to leave."

"So what's the problem? Maybe people don't want their picture taken after a wreck. I know I wouldn't."

"I didn't see anything wrong with it."

"Why are here so early anyway? Didn't you have to work tonight?"

"Yeah. I went to work but the manager didn't like my ugly nail polish and told me to leave."

"You're probably not allowed to even wear nail polish. You should just go to your room and take it off so you won't get sent home again for that."

And off he goes. He just seemed to get more headstrong everyday.

***

On the 13th, Cameron received a Warning from the Denton County Sheriff's Department for Speeding/Nonsafe. He was lucky that time. I do not know how much over the speed limit he was driving.

On the 19th, Cameron received yet another ticket. This time

it was for speeding and not using a seat belt. He/we sent in the payment and plead "guilty or no contest."

***

In order to be prepared for graduation day, I talked to Cameron's school counselor and got his spring schedule. I decided to be hard on him to make sure he passed everything. I had to try a different strategy.

The week of Thanksgiving my manager insisted my sarcasm is too much for him. So I spoke to a HR person but she took his side. Things were not looking good there as I applied for other positions there but nothing was coming through for me.

Turkey Day – I cooked a 15-pound turkey and the boys wanted to eat at the breakfast table; they didn't like eating at the "big table" in our formal dining room. We also had one of Cameron's favorites, yams with pineapple and pecans. Dan carved the turkey as usual.

We gorged on all the delicious food and then went our separate ways in the house. Cameron to his room, Dan to the garage, and I went to the loft to work on greeting cards on my computer. We all had a relaxing day, which we needed.

My therapist told me that I am Cameron's enabler and I must go to Al-Anon meetings. I went to one and I was told that I shouldn't continue to put up with my son's ways. This way of thinking was not for me. I suppose I was an enabler in that case.

I took Cameron to a new psychologist, Dr. Rasile. I suggested that perhaps Cameron had ADHD; I thought that might be part of his problem. The preliminary reports suggested that he didn't have that but the psychologist needed to see all of his school records first. I gathered them up from Raleigh schools and from Nannette because he lived with them for a few years.

Since I requested something from Nanette, she took the opportunity to let me know about Cameron's blog posts. I knew about the posts but they were mostly him just rambling. True, I didn't read all of them.

She was just concerned about him. Aren't we all? I felt like everyone was accusing me of being a bad mom, but I didn't know what else to do.

According to my journal, I spend a lot of time shopping to ease my mental angst during this time. The Dallas area was a shopping mecca, so there were plenty of options to sooth myself.

DECEMBER 2004

Cameron saw Dr. Rasile on a regular basis – bi-weekly. They talked about J.C.'s death, Cameron's addictions, and more, but not Cameron's sexual identity problem, which concerned me.

Cameron noted in his blog after his first meeting with her that after telling her his entire history – again (he'd done this several times by now) that he was depressed. However, he liked her because she listened to him. Funny how I didn't like her much, but she wasn't my therapist so I kept my feelings to myself.

I spoke with Dr. Rasile on the phone, prior to Cameron's next appointment, regarding Cameron's possible sexual identity issue. She suggested that I confront him at the next session with my questions.

After Cameron's session with Dr. Rasile, she called me into her office while Cameron was still there.

"Mom, you said you wanted to discuss something with Cameron. Would you like to start?

"Sure. Cameron, I'm concerned about you thinking you're gay. Are you?"

Cameron glared at me and said, "It's none of your business."

He got up and left for school after that and the doctor didn't say anything. So I said, "good bye" and left as well. That was a strange ending but I don't recall any conclusion from the doctor. Perhaps she assumed that Cameron had said what he wanted and that was the end of that.

My concern came after Cameron's brief relationship with the guy named Kelly during the past summer. I thought, since he was having so many problems with girls that adding in a guy would just make matters worse, not better. As there was no conclusion, I kept my fingers crossed that he would survive all of his relationships. I wasn't going to tell him he couldn't see a guy; I was merely concerned. Moreover, he mentioned to me the past year that he thought he might be bisexual. I think saying something about his sexuality twice indicated to me that he had a concern himself and needed help with it. Guess I was wrong.

***

To keep my sanity, I volunteered for various activities – at Nokia and with the Texas Outdoor Women's Network (TOWN) group that I belonged to; I enjoyed taking advantage of all that Texas had to offer. I enjoyed the outings that TOWN offered such as meeting up and going to the Dallas Arboretum as well as camping trips in Texas and beyond. I had planned trips for the groups to go "eagle hunting" as well as a rafting trip on the Brazos River.

***

Towards the middle of the month – it was December after all - I was getting antsy about our little family not being in the Christmas spirit. I finally got Dan to go with me to get a real tree. We put up it in the front room so everyone in the neighborhood could see it. Dan didn't put any lights up outside that year. Our house was like a war zone, or so it seemed at times.

Dan helped put lights on the tree and Cameron hung our special ornaments sans balls. We were not in a very Christmas-y-happy mood this year due to Cameron's current mood and his exploitations. At least having the Christmas tree lights made the house a bit more festive.

Cameron mentioned in a blog post that two great things about Christmas were the movies "How the Grinch Stole Christmas" and "The Nightmare Before Christmas." He was not overly fond of the holiday season.

***

Cameron received a warning from the Flower Mound court about a ticket he received in November. Cameron told us that he thought it was a warning rather than an actual ticket. Dan yelled me at for not telling him about the ticket but I was just tired of him being mad about Cameron all the time.

His ticket was for driving 33 mph in a 22 mph school zone and not wearing a seatbelt. The ticket price had increased to $663!

***

I worked from home the week between Christmas and New Year's, which was a relief since my manager and I weren't getting along. I started to get excited about our trip back to North Carolina and Wisconsin to visit our families.

Cameron's next appointment with Dr. Rasile was about setting up a budget, since Cameron had blown through most of his savings account paying off tickets. Cameron was upset about this and left crying.

> I stepped back in to talk to her about this and she stated, "You need to stop being Cameron's "big sister" and be his mom."

She also called me on my nervous giggle. I told you I didn't like her!

Before we started Christmas celebrations and traveling, we had to figure out how to pay Cameron's latest ticket. The court was closed for the holidays and I wasn't sure if Cameron had money in his account to pay the ticket.

Dan offered to pay for it until Cameron's Social Security check hit the bank. They decided to write a letter to the court explaining everything and then we mailed it but there was nothing else we could do. That ordeal was stressful for us as were trying to keep Cameron from possibly going to jail.

We all went to the Christmas Eve service at Triest Lutheran

Church. This was the church Cameron's best friend went to; I'm sure Cameron was hoping to see Everett there but he didn't. Cameron still missed his company but Everett's mom forbade Cameron from going to their house since he continued to do drugs.

Christmas Day – we woke Cameron up at 10:00 a.m. so we could eat and open presents. Everyone was happy with their gifts, I received a Canon ELPH camera, Cameron got new tires for his car, and Dan got an angle grinder, among other items.

Cameron gave me some strange gifts. One was a smallish white bear with a hard on. Really! He thought it was great but I was a bit embarrassed by it.

He also gave me a candleholder and wrote this note to go with it...

> Mother,
>
> I am aware this appears to be used an ashtray perhaps? I saw it and thought it might be cool for holding giant candles. Or at least holding something...it's so pretty!
>
> (a picture of heart) Cameron
>
> I am also aware that these are not giant candles in this particular assortment. But I assumed that I'd screw up and pick a nasty-smelling one. These 3 little ones smell good though. Okay, enough writing...

I loved getting little notes from my son. He really was insightful.

We spent the remainder of the day munching on Christmas ham and junk food.

***

Since we were headed to Wisconsin and it's generally very cold in December there, I took Cameron out shopping the next day for some warm clothes. He only picked out one shirt he liked and it wasn't really for cold weather.

Dan and I took Sheila to Fireplug Inn, a boarding place for pets, to stay while we were traveling. She liked it there but we were sad when we got home because she wasn't there. Pets can really calm a household down – to a certain extent.

The following day, I went to the Penney's Outlet at Grapevine Mills and bought myself a warm jacket and sweaters for Dan and Cameron. I was determined to get Cameron some warm clothes for this trip!

We flew to Milwaukee on Monday for a two-day visit with Dan's mom, and his brothers' families. Cameron seemed to just want to sleep when it was time to visit Dan's family. We left him a couple of times because he just wasn't pleasant to be around. Pictures I took of him showed him with a very red nose and red cheeks along with half closed eyes. I don't know what kind of drugs he was doing, but it didn't make for a pleasant trip for Dan and I. His lack of enthusiasm was embarrassing for me.

After the Milwaukee visit, we flew to Raleigh to see my family and we stayed in a hotel not to put anyone out. We stayed three days visiting my mom and dad, sisters and nieces and nephews. We had a tradition of having a shrimp boil during this time of year and we did it that year as well. Dan loved it! It was held at my sister Kristie's house and their house was full with everyone there.

Cameron was again, being very distant. He was the definition of depressed. Once again he had the look of someone either very sick or doing some type of drug. It doesn't seem that it would be meth because he was so sleepy all the time. I asked if he was sick and he said "no".

While we were out, Cameron received phone calls on his mobile from people he didn't know. He would tell them that he was in North Carolina, so he couldn't help them but I had a feeling he was dealing meth again and his friends would have known he was out of town.

So it seemed Cameron had fallen off the wagon and was not longer clean and sober. He was probably using and dealing drugs at that time but only time would tell.

Before heading back to Texas, Dan and I drove Cameron to Rocky Mount so he could spend the rest of his school holiday with Nanette and Julia. One of their friends met us to take him to Washington and Cameron was on his way to the next leg of travel.

We got back home on January 2, just in time to pick up Sheila from the boarders. We were as happy to see her just as she was to see us, too. This little dog was the highlight of our lives now.

JANUARY 2005

Cameron returned from his visit to his sister and stepmom's with a piercing on his face. It's located between his lower lip and chin. Since he did not get my approval, nor was he 18, I told him to remove the stud.

His retort, "But it was a gift from Nannette!"

"I don't care. You didn't get my permission."

He reluctantly removed the piercing. Thank goodness, I hated seeing his face with a piercing. By now, he had many piercing in his ears and ear lobes. That started when he was 16, I didn't mind the ear piercings so much, as that was the norm for teens and young adults but a facial piercing was going too far in my mind.

I think he pierced his ears himself or had one of his girlfriends help him. He probably enjoyed the pain involved.

When Cameron started back to school for his last semester in school, he wouldn't be in School Newspaper, or at Dale Jackson. That must had been a shock to his very being because he loved both so much.

I found this blog post Cameron wrote early in January...

> "...I am having a lot of trouble not being in newspaper. For some reason, the last two days been somewhat haunting to me. I keep thinking of all the old classes I had. And the fact that highschool is so close to being over. Don't misunderstand; I still hate how highschool is managed and am ecstatic that I'm going to be moving on, to a more mature method of education, but something about all the people I've come across, and all the friends I've made, even all the people I've hated looking at…it's so close to over. I am having trouble dealing with it. I know it sounds lame, and I always laughed at others when they said this same shit, but, wow, years of my life, spending

uncountable all-nighters finishing up papers, causing scenes, seeing how much I could get away with, making English teachers feel stupid for using shitty grammar...I just really don't want to leave it. But at the same time, I'm glad I'll finally be able to make decisions for myself. That is always a plus. I don't need the fuckin' attendance clerks to call my mommy and daddy to get me in trouble for making a personal decision. I am finally going to be in charge, both legally and personally, of what I do every day. It's the biggest and greatest present anyone could ever give m me.

I don't understand senioritis. Apparently it hits a lot of kids, especially about this time of year. I, on the other hand, spent freshman, sophomore and junior year living very calmly...it's just school after all. But, this year is probably the first since 6th grade that I am actually striving to do well. Weird, I'd say. ..."

Sounds as if he's maturing.

***

Back at my job, I had several interviews attempting to move into a different position but I was asked to go to Human Resources again. It seemed they wanted me to leave the company with a severance package. I knew things weren't going well with my latest boss. His personality and mine clashed too much.

So I had that stress to manage as well as the Cameron stress. At that point, I was seeing a therapist and Cameron was seeing a psychologist. My visits helped me deal with both Cameron and Dan to a certain extent. Life was still difficult for all of us.

***

Cameron's last visit with Dr. Rasile was on January 22; she had released him from her care. He probably should have kept going to see her, especially since he liked her, but I never inquired about the cost of going once the insurance ran out.

Cameron had started seeing a psychiatrist regularly around this time as well. This month he had given Cameron Abilify to try to level out his moods. He was also taking Lexapro.

Dan and I had started talking about moving back to North Carolina. My parents were getting older, we had many friends there, and there wasn't a reason to remain in Texas after Cameron graduated. I hoped that we could get him lined up to attend a college nearby in North Texas. He had so many friends in Texas that we didn't think he would want to leave them at this point.

Thinking on all this, I never asked Cameron what he wanted to do. I assumed he would want to stay and go to college in Texas.

We had a realtor come over to look at our house so we could start getting it ready to sell. It seemed so soon to be talking to a realtor but this was our plan for the next year or so. Dan was already allowed to work from home with his job that was based in California, so they said it wouldn't matter if he did the same in North Carolina. It was time to move forward with our plan.

FEBRUARY 2005

February 2 - Cameron had a reaction to a cold medicine and his prescribed medications. I gave him some medicine not knowing that he'd have a reaction. He called me from school saying his head kept going to one side.

This scared the bejesus out of me! I picked him up from school and methodically tried to figure out whom to call to fix this and make sure it was not something serious.

I first called the pharmacist and he thought it would be best to see our family doctor since it could be meningitis. I called our family doctor; they said to come in. I also called his psychiatrist, since he prescribed the meds.

Dr. Zrnic, Cameron's psychiatrist, recommended giving Cameron a Benadryl and see if that helped. While we were waiting at the doctor's office, Cameron got extremely sleepy and was better but the doctor still wanted to see him to be sure it wasn't meningitis, since the symptoms are similar. His doctor marked down that Cameron had Acute Sinusitis, Dizziness, Headache, and Tremor.

It wasn't meningitis and the Benadryl was the answer to the situation. Cameron was so sweet when he needed my help, such as in this case. He was truly a Gemini – acting two different ways all the time!

I received a severance package from Nokia to mull over, but in the meantime, I headed off to Lake Buchanan in the Texas mountains to go eagle hunting! I had planned this trip for the TOWN group, so there was no way I wasn't going. I thought the trip would relieve some pressure from my stressed life.

After I got back from my relaxing trip, I officially resigned from Nokia (I was technically forced out) but this set me on a path of depression. I'm sure all the stress at home did not make me a very happy employee, so it was for the best.

Even though I lost a job that I had liked so much, I was much more relaxed at home now. I could turn my focus back on my husband and child, and getting the house ready to sell.

We hadn't seen much of Cameron this month. His car was broken for a while so he had friends taking him here and there.

Kelly took Cameron out on Valentine's Day. I didn't hear how it went but it was sweet for her to take him out. Perhaps she was trying to get back in his good graces, he had broken up with her, or so we thought.

I found out that Cameron has been skipping days from school due to some girlfriend issues again. If only the girls would leave him alone and let him finish high school!

MARCH 2005

Cameron started the month off with another violation. This time for, "Wrong/False name on request" given by the school police officer. This was a $187 offense.

The officer seemed a bit over-enthused with handing out tickets to students – or at least to Cameron. He seemed to have it out for Cameron since he also presented tickets for smoking a cigarette off campus more than once and yelling an obscenity in public while at school. I'm sure the judge also thought these was ridiculous.

Cameron was able to be friends with most everyone else at

Marcus, but not "Officer Bob". I sure would have liked to have met this man back then and ask him what he had against my son.

Dan and I had grown weary of making sure Cameron went to court for all his violations so this one slipped past us – or perhaps we didn't know about it until a letter from the Flower Mound Municipal Court showed up with a court date, April 4, 2005 at 10:00 am. It was for a plea hearing.

Note: Cameron did not make his court date in April.

In addition, earlier in the month we received a letter from Cameron's school regarding his attendance record. Apparently, Cameron had missed too many days of class so we were getting a letter stating that Cameron report to school immediately in compliance with the law. What?!?

The stress that I was experiencing from my job situation was no doubt a part of the problems at home. I have since learned that when it's in the home, your children will experience stress and depression as well. Dan was probably experiencing work pressure as well, and he was working from home – and upstairs where Cameron's room was. Therefore, if the two of them were upstairs at the same time, then Cameron would listen to Dan's rants and raves about work issues.

Yet, I don't remember him having many work problems after we moved back to North Carolina in August 2006.

I was escaping the situation on a regular basis by taking trips here and there. Perhaps if Cameron could have escaped more on school trips or something similar, he might have pulled through. But I know that drugs were his escape and his downfall.

Stress just brings aggression and aggravation into a home. Our home was like a battlefield for at least two years. I feel certain that there are many homes where a teen is present and it's the same or at least, similar story.

Sure, we had good times together as a family but when meth became Cameron's best friend, there were none that I can remember. I feel Cameron would have preferred to live a normal life but he got a caught up in the excitement of a drug dealer life during this last year.

He seemed to brag about his adventures of getting the drugs and then taking them back to his friends. Maybe there's a sense of responsibility there, or perhaps it was more the ability to be able to do the drug himself whenever he wanted to.

I do hate drugs, though. They have brought down so many good people.

What drives people to do drugs? Generally, something in their life they want to escape. What if they are cursed with having an addictive gene in their body? Well then, we should do everything possible to prevent them from ever starting to drink or do drugs.

I don't believe there was a direct history of addiction in mine or Cameron's father's history, but maybe, J.C. was adopted so we didn't know the genetics of his blood parents.

One of my grandfathers was an alcoholic and my other grandfather killed himself when I was a baby but my parents did not drink or abuse drugs.

I believe Cameron's addiction problems stemmed from his father's death – plain and simple.

APRIL 2005

Cameron was active in Skills USA due to Mrs. Harmon's urging in his Graphic Design class. I found a newsletter in which he was mentioned for winning a blue ribbon in Ad Design. Kelly also won a blue ribbon in Ad Design.

Cameron never bragged about these accomplishments. I discovered that the blue ribbon was for an ad with photos of ballerinas that was so graceful and beautiful. It hangs on a wall in my current home – with the blue ribbon. He truly had talent.

I gave Cameron a mail off drug test. It came back in the mail positive for methamphetamine and amphetamine. I didn't think he was still clean and I hated that.

We did another one a couple of weeks later and it was positive for TCP (marijuana) but I doubted that it was his urine sample. I questioned it because Lauren was at the house the day I tested him. That just sounded like something they would do. Neither he nor she were clean - bottom line.

Since I wasn't working anymore, I tried selling my Car Cards to bring in a little money. I also did trailer checks at local theaters, which didn't bring in much money either but I enjoyed it all the same. I could escape reality while watching the latest movies and for free. My job was to write down all the ads and trailers before selected movies. I took Cameron on many of these jobs in years past.

I was able to go the gym and take Pilates classes as well as lift weights, two things I loved doing. At least then, I had the time. Of course it wasn't free so I went while I could still afford it. Working out or doing some physical activity helps a person mentally as well as physically.

I was depressed for many reasons: no job, my husband and son argue all the time, and I had to see that Cameron graduated some how! He was my focus then.

Dan took a trip to Wisconsin, since his mother was not well. This allowed Cameron some freedom since it was always tense when the two of them were in the house at the same time.

April 27 Cameron writes in his blog the following:

> "I wake up this morning and get ready for school... psch. In other words, I roll out of bed and kinda put shoes on. I go downstairs and open the envelope from UNT that has been sitting, waiting for me to open it, on the counter for two or three days. It was from admission, so I knew what it contained...but didn't at the same time. I open it only to be denied by the only thing I was actually looking forward to in the near future. No UNT for Cameron...at least not full-time. I'm sure I could still go part-time, but it's just not quite the same. So this obliviously put a major damper on my mood from the very beginning. But I felt no need to bring others down, so I simply carried on trying not be too depressed about it."

The letter from UNT was not a surprise to me but I hated seeing Cameron's disappointment. They included with the rejection letter information about the "Deferred Scholar Program", which Cameron could apply for.

It had several stipulations:
- » Enroll in the program no later than September 1, 2005
- » Complete 12 hours of transferable core-course hours at

another institution with a 2.5 GPA between high school graduation and the end of the fall 2005 semester.
» Participate in at least 3 Student Success activities during the Fall 2005 semester.
» Complete a monthly progress summary with the Office of New Student and Mentoring Programs
» Attend University Orientation for Deferred Scholars in January 2006
» Enroll in the University of North Texas for the Spring 2006 semester

He agreed to enroll in this program so we faxed in his information form on May 8, 2005. He was accepted on June 30. His next step was to register at a community college.

It would be a waste for him to not go to college since his grandfather had left a trust fund just for that purpose.

***

He started to mention a riff going on with Lauren and Kelly – they don't know each other yet and they are both jealous of each other. They both wanted Cameron.

The same day, he wrote about his appointment with his psychiatrist and the "love" issue:

> "...he gave me stratera to help me concentrate...I need that right now, especially with this bullshit I'm currently dealing with outside of school. It's sad that my extracurricular activity is fighting the battle of love. Almost enough to make someone want to

squeeze the trigger, listen for the click and suck on that sweet, sweet lead. Anyways, the doc appointment wasn't so bad, but I'm glad it was as short as it was."

***

Cameron wrote a blog post on April 28, 2005 about his issues with Kelly:

> "Gah, Kelly is freaking me out. She actually threatened that if we got back together in the future that I wouldn't be able to leave. Like...she'd kill me. It's one thing to joke about that, but she was completely serious...."

At the end of the month, Cameron had another car accident with Lauren. She was driving and Cameron pulled the steering wheel causing the car to jump the curb and run into a brick wall on Valley Parkway in Lewisville.

I'll set the scene first; Cameron had slept most of Saturday after going to a local concert. He had a great time with friends while listening to two bands. He decided he wanted to see Lauren, since the previous night went so well with her. He forgot to take his meds but figured everything would be okay.

They get together and Lauren was in a pissed off mood. Cameron wrote:

> "I'm not sure exactly what I did to piss her off...but it must have been bad. She then asked me to fight her.
>
> I know that it's wrong to fight females...but something told me that it would be okay to this time.

I wasn't going to be violent, just heavily playful so that she'd get some kind of challenge. We got out of the car and into the grass...and I could tell she was pissed and need to let out anger. So I pushed her back to start it. And off it went. But something weird happened inside of me. All the shit I've been going though lately, all this bullshit, all the girl problems...I just wanted to beat the shit out of her for ever bring this upon me (which isn't her fault... but when someone is hitting you, it doesn't become a question who to drop the blame on.) So, earlier on, I had been taking a lot of hits, then just shoving her back decently hard. But the more hits I took the more I wanted to just make her limp. So I started throwing her to the ground. And even picked her up and threw her at one point. And, at one point, which I feel really bad about, I kicked her in the ass while she was on the ground because I was so pissed. I never actually hit her, but I know what I did must have hurt like hell. She did well too, however. My jaw still hurts from where she hit me in the face... must have been a nice hit. So, after the fight, both us were really pissed. And I jumped out of the car while we were about to leave and started walking home...but she picked me up and made me take her...

We kept arguing, and she got a few tears and a scream out of me. I had already lost my mind and was just listening to her lecture me. I grabbed the steering wheel and pulled it down. We skidded off the road into a brick wall. At this point, I was pissed beyond caring. It took about ten minutes for me to realize exactly what I had done. I tried apologizing, I tried comforting her, but it was too late. She's scared of me now. I never wanted this to happen. I always knew that I could be terrible if driven far enough. But I'm still very sad and sorry that it had to happen to her.

Cops came, parents came, and so did my past tickets that I forgot about. I was arrested right there on the side of the street. First time in jail...how exciting. So, I sat in handcuffs for about 2-3 hours, waiting for the drunks in front of me to get booked in. I've never been so pissed at drunks. So, I got booked in, they gave me a blanket, and I basically slept the whole time...time flew by very fast, actually. My mother bailed me out...most of the money was my own, anyways, so she didn't complain about how much it cost. I went home and slept the whole day.

What a shitty weekend. I can't keep talking about it because it's making me cry...and I know that sounds lame...but I really feel terrible for everything that happened. Well, I'll write more another time.

Sometime.

Good night.

Cameron"

Our side of the story:

Cameron called and asked us to go to the accident scene (it's after midnight), actually, Lauren's parents asked him to call us. We did and saw a cracked windshield on his side (he said it was a boom box that hit the windshield). Later, Dan and I figured that it was more likely his head hit the windshield, as he wasn't wearing a seat belt, but we weren't concerned at the time since there was no blood.

While we were there talking with Lauren's parents and the Lewisville police, the police discovered that Cameron had two warrants out for his arrest; one for failure to appear and the second for the Failure to ID given in April (remember – I wrote he didn't go to court). His bond was set at $542 for both offenses.

Cameron was handcuffed and taken off to jail. Lauren was hysterical.

We left Cameron in jail for the evening, since he didn't bother to take care of his ticket. I had mixed emotions about the whole ordeal. I remembered him receiving notices about this ticket but Cameron thought it was just a warning.

I didn't sleep well for obvious reasons. My son was in jail. I guess it was only a matter of time, but the reason was so absurd! Not the Failure to Appear in court but the failure to identify himself. I'm sure that Officer Bob knew who Cameron was by now.

Officer Bob ---- whatever! Hope your retirement is going well.

I bailed Cameron out in the morning. He had most of the fine money in his bank account so I withdrew it on the way to the Lewisville police station. Paying the bond closed out the violations.

Cameron did not enjoy his jail experience – imagine! He said he spent most of the time in a hallway because some drunken guys were being booked before him.

As I write this, I do sound a bit like an overprotective mother in some ways. Isn't this in our genes, to protect our children? I also felt freedom was important to a teenager. I surely didn't have all the answers. I'm not sure if I had any of the answers. I do know that Cameron was a gentleman and was concerned for other's feelings. He did not physically hurt anyone. He cared about the human soul and psyche. He was wise beyond his years in many ways and immature in other ways. Many of his friends looked up to Cameron, which I found interesting. Dan and I saw the bad side of Cameron for the most part for the past two years while his friends got to spend more time with him that was probably the "fun Cameron."

I later read a poem he wrote about the fight and the ensuing accident:

Whimsical toss by the waterfall

Secular ways of the breeze.

Irrational, offset and screwed

As her fingers bounce from the keys.

With a crash into a solid brick wall,

And screaming at top of my lung

The night's chaos finally unwinding,

But the misery only begun.

Her tears flowing on, everlasting,

Realization of what I proposed.

And now I fear my subconscious,

Whose wicked actions arose.
I am not very violent at all;
Neither malice nor tyrannical hate.
Thought I laid ravenous hands upon her,
I hope love won't arrive too late.
I love without question or comment
But always with a delicate whisper.
And never again shall I touch that child
Unless she allow that I kiss her.
So sweet her touch and delicate,
Like rose petal upon one's lips.
And so calm her voice, it soothes my mind,
Causing reality to slip.
I don't know why I harmed this girl...
No reason yet discovered.
Yet I hope she will forgive and believe me
When I say I love her.

MAY 2005

I found another poem Cameron wrote after the fight and accident which affected him more than I knew:

May 2, 2005

Days diminishing, no work to be done.

My life it seems pointless

The assholes here won.

I want to die.

No more, no less
To stop this shit
And end this quest.
An empty journey
Through dead terrain...
I found my solace,
To end my pain.
Take a knife
Against my vein
Press and pull
To spill the pain.

Apparently the fight with Lauren has touched his soul deeply as well as the visit in jail.

Cameron wrote to Erin, dated May 3, 2005. It seems he never mailed it to her. Below are some highlights of the letter, which reveal how he was thinking and feeling that month:

> All I can say is that I'm almost done with school, I'm sick of being in Texas, and I've stopped caring about most things. I went to jail Saturday night. That was a new experience. I'm going to try to keep that from being a habit. Soon I'll need to find a place to live... how shitty. So, I'd say that things are going shitilly (fun to say), but I don't want to complain...I've begun not caring about so many things. I'm wondering if I could just move to New York after I graduate... This obviously isn't the greatest idea, but then... I don't really care. I fully intend on going to college, but perhaps I should take a year to learn to live by

myself first. I dunno...But I'm taking a break from writing a smidge...Thy wrist hurteth.

No, I didn't read this letter until after his death, but what would I have done differently? He was already seeing a psychologist and psychiatrist.

***

Back to school issues: I checked with Cameron's teachers to see what else needed to happen to make sure he would graduate.

I found out that he needed to complete a couple of papers for History and English – let's make it happen!

I explained in a letter to Cameron that, he had been going to school since he was 5 years old and it would be silly to throw it all away now. It seemed to have worked as he focused on getting everything completed by time to be approved for graduation!

Before graduation, I took a trip to Raleigh to go house hunting. It was getting closer to reality now. I had a hard time finding just the right location. I also snuck in a trip to Wrightsville Beach with mom, Kristie and Kelly. I remember us watching an episode of "Intervention" (the show about drug addicts and their interventions). It was focused on meth users. It was sad to think my son was similar to the guy in the show. We talked a little bit about it during the show.

My sister asked, "Cameron's into that right?"

"Yep, I'm afraid so."

We were all quiet while watching.

2004 - 2005 Senior Year

Fortunately, Cameron stayed out of trouble while I was gone.

***

I made a deal with Cameron that if he worked hard to graduate, passed all his classes, and was approved to graduate, then his friend Erin could come visit for his birthday and graduation (like he needed another female in this life!). Dan was not happy about this proposal.

That was the impetus to get his butt in gear.

On May 25, Cameron's teachers said he had met all the requirements and could graduate! YAY!

Erin arrived from upstate New York a couple of days before graduation. As we were also expecting my mom and sister to come for the big occasion, the guest bedroom downstairs was taken over by them. Therefore, I let Erin stay upstairs in the craft room on an air mattress.

The craft room was a bedroom in reality so there was plenty of room for a queen size air mattress but Erin didn't seem to mind the space at all. I felt it was best to give her a place to hang some clothes and be able to close the door. I knew it was somewhat risky to have them both upstairs but I felt okay about it.

Cameron was pretty excited about graduating! He didn't show lots of excitement but having Erin in town and graduating brought a smile to his face. I had missed seeing him smile for the past few years. Smiles were few and far between.

My sister, Kristie, and mother flew in from North Carolina for Cameron's birthday and graduation, the day before. They could tell how happy I was for Cameron. They were as well.

MAY 28, 2005 GRADUATION!

Cameron graduated the day before his 18th birthday!

Graduation! I was so happy! Cameron appeared happy as well.

The ceremony was held at University of North Texas Coliseum in Denton, a 35-minute drive north from Flower Mound.

Cameron left early to line up and do whatever it is you do when you graduate (I've forgotten). Erin rode along with him. Dan, Mom, Kristie, and I, all piled into my car and headed to Denton to watch Cameron receive his high school diploma. Little did I know, that would be the last graduation and shining moment in his life.

The coliseum at UNT was huge. Cameron's class was 775 strong so this was the appropriate size to hold all the well-wishers of family and friends. No tickets were required to attend.

We had hoped to see Cameron before the ceremony started. The Marcus colors were red and black, so the Class of 2005 wore red gowns along with red caps. It was a sea of red trying to find him.

We managed to spot him before he had to line up. He looked fantastic wearing a muted green dress shirt, brown patterned tie, black pants, and black dress shoes.

Cameron also had a black cord around his neck signifying his artistic ability. I was surprised that he was being honored but that made me ever more proud.

When I saw him I asked, "What's the cord for?"

"For my artistic achievements or something like that" he said shrugging his shoulders.

He probably knew about getting this but never bragged about it. His low self-esteem kept kicking him back to the curb.

I was so nervous for some reason that night. I suppose it was just a big night and I was super proud of my son!

Erin and Lauren found us and sat in the row in front of us. Kelly didn't come – probably too many girlfriends already attending. Leave it to Cameron to have three girlfriends!

As our entourage of six watched the seniors march in, I frantically searched for Cameron. I was so excited about Cameron graduating that I wanted to capture every moment with my camera. Once I spotted him, I started taking pictures and Lauren videotaped the event.

We had a long wait until they finally started calling out the "S" names, but Jace Cameron Stephenson was finally called and I took pictures of his every step.

Of course, I was too far away to get a good picture but I kept trying, which meant that I didn't really watch him walk across the stage – damn it! (Now I try to remember to turn off the photographer inside me and be a part of the moment instead).

Fortunately, I found out later that the entire ceremony was video recorded by the school – something else Cameron failed to share with me and they had a professional photographer taking pictures of all the graduates.

After the ceremony, the coliseum was bubbling with excitement. We tried earnestly to find our new graduate afterward. We called him on his phone but when we tried to describe where we were, we couldn't, because there were no real landmarks. We gave up and headed to my car.

Cameron popped up out of nowhere and surprised us in the

parking lot. He was so happy! I gave him a big hug congratulating him on his achievement.

It started to sprinkle and was dark by then but I insisted on getting some photos of the two of us, with him wearing his gown. I asked Kristie to take some pictures of us. Unfortunately, these are not the best photos but they are all I have and I'll cherish them forever.

> I asked him before we parted ways, "What did you do with your cap?"
>
> Cameron sensed where I was going with this said, "I threw it in the air but don't worry, I took the tassel off first" smiling while showing me his red tassel with a gold stamped "2005" dangling off it.

Cameron had a fetish for tassels and now he had his own. He wanted mine from when I graduated from NCSU so I let him borrow it. He was there, after all. That was in 1996 and he was nine years old.

As he didn't want any special recognition at home, he went his way with Erin and we headed back to Flower Mound, stopping at the Cotton Patch to eat a late dinner. Sometimes I wished I had done something special for him anyway, because he and Erin didn't do much afterward either.

***

Getting Cameron to see the light and get his butt in gear so he could graduate with his fellow classmates was a challenge, but it was one I was glad I conquered. Although he wasn't ready for the changes coming up in his life – college, loss of friends and maybe the loss of his parents who were moving away and leaving him there. This realization hurts me the most.

Honestly, we thought we were doing the right thing and quite frankly, Cameron's drug use had worn us down. We were ready for a change, but not the one that was to occur later in the summer.

Cameron had graduated from high school and was preparing for the next phase of his life – or was he?

CAMERON IS AN ADULT NOW

AN ADULT IS BORN – MAY 29, 2005

Cameron turned 18, officially an adult now and legally able to make his own life decisions. I wish he could have made better choices, but I also feel that he had far more grief and depression than the average teenager did. It was more than he could handle.

We took everyone to Pappadeaux Seafood Kitchen for his birthday lunch. That was our favorite celebratory restaurant and Dan and I were eager to take Kristie and Mom there. Erin went as well.

Cameron was extremely down that day. He only ordered calamari at the restaurant and when I wanted to get some group shoots after lunch, he was so sour-faced that it hurt me. Everyone else was smiling except the birthday boy.

We gave him some simple gifts for graduation and his birthday. Kristie brought him a couple of bizarre posters and an interesting tie.

I went to Target with Mom and Kristie the day they arrived to look for some fun gifts for Cameron. I thought a cookbook would be cool for him since he always showed an interest in cooking. He got his very own Betty Crocker cookbook for his 18th birthday!

He was fascinated with my cookbook, in which I had collected recipes for a long time. All the recipes in it were handwritten, as they were all "keepers." The recipes were mostly ones that Dan and Cameron really liked, as well as cookie and cake recipes that I liked.

He said once, "And to think one day, that cookbook will be mine."

Dan was generous and gave Cameron the title to the Taurus that he had been driving for the past 8 months.

The afternoon of his birthday Cameron and Erin took off to see friends. I'm not sure what he did but I left the afternoon and evening up to him, as it was his birthday.

That evening I went up to upstairs to see what Cameron and Erin were up to. I found them both asleep in his bed – fully clothed. They looked so happy together that I just let them be.

***

My sister and mom headed home the next day. They had to get back to their lives but it was great to have so many people in our house.

Cameron wanted to show Erin Lake Grapevine, which was close by. That was a favored hangout spot for Cameron and his friends. They were driving along the small road beside the lake and a man pulled out into Cameron's car. They were both okay but the car was not. What a way to end a great weekend.

The car was totaled but the accident wasn't his fault this time.

We called a wrecker to get the car from the lake back to our house. Dan wanted to look at it and see if he could repair it. Plus, the insurance company would need to look at it to determine if it was totaled or not.

The accident was a real downer for Cameron. He was very sad about the loss of his first car, "Delilah."

Erin returned home to New York the next day. Cameron was really depressed then. His car was totaled and then Erin was gone as well.

JUNE 2005

Since it was the other driver's fault, we received insurance money for Cameron's totaled Taurus. The three of us ensued on a used car hunt but Cameron didn't care about getting another car. He was depressed and was again, using meth for recreation.

We found a nice looking, pewter 1995 Altima in good condition – or so we thought. The car was purchased in Cameron's name.

We had lots of problems with that car: axels breaking, battery dying, tires going flat. It left Cameron stranded many times but he learned how to change a tire, fix a battery, and ask for help. I liked that he was taking all this on himself. He asked Dan what to do about the latest problem and he'd offer his advice.

Cameron had successfully graduated from high school and now needed to find another job, so he doesn't sleep his life away.

I suggested some job ideas to him; he applied and got a job with RGIS, an inventory company. He was required to drive to various locations in the Dallas metroplex. For some crazy reason, he chose the early morning shift, which was not a good idea.

He loved the aspect of going to different places and the inventory part was easy. Yet, he overslept twice and lost that job! Therefore, it was back to job hunting again.

Things were rough with Cameron's lack of enthusiasm. When he worked, he would come home and sleep for the rest of the day.

We had suspicions that he was doing meth again.

I was tired of dealing with him and Dan. What change needed to occur to make our home happy again? Maybe I should have left with Cameron or sent him to live in North Carolina with his stepmom and sister. I should have made some kind of change! Yet, I didn't have the finances to do anything.

Cameron turned some kind of page just after his 18th birthday and graduation. He decided he was tired of being told what to do and how to live his life so he plunged headlong into the dusky world of meth, or ice, which he preferred. (The difference between ice and other methamphetamines is that ice undergoes additional refinement to remove impurities).

I knew he was changing that summer and I even called him on it. I wanted him to go back to rehab so I could have my happy Cameron back and so he could carry on with his life, but he knew I could not commit him to a rehab facility without his approval since he was now 18 so said, "No way."

Cameron was not taking showers, he was not brushing his teeth, and he was just barely tolerable.

His eating habits had changed. He used to eat dinners with us, but now he had somewhere he had to be conveniently when it was time for dinner. His meals consisted of Pop Tarts (frozen), Ramon noodles (sometimes), ice cream, anything sweet he could get his hands on, and soft drinks, which he drank like water.

I have read that meth addicts crave sweets and that sure fit Cameron over that summer. I once found him finishing off a half gallon of sugar free ice cream, that really wasn't very good, but he ate the last three quarters of it anyway. That was a lot of ice cream!

Meth seemed to have taken its toll on his memory as well. One night we asked him to unload the dishwasher, which was one of his chores. He opened the dishwasher and then walked away. He had totally forgotten to do it.

Another night, he went into the bathroom, turned on the shower, and went back into his room forgetting that the water was running. I urged him to take a shower as he was looking grungy with oily hair and he was dirty from skateboarding.

As I was sitting at my desk in the loft, I noticed that the shower ran quite a long time without Cameron in it. I eventually knocked on his bedroom door and asked him about it. He said he had done that to try to fool me into thinking that he was taking a shower but I think he forgot.

He was secretly dating both Kelly and Lauren during the summer. Dan and I knew about this and encouraged him to pick one or the other because it wasn't fair to them for him to be involved with both and it was making him a bit crazy. In his journal, he explained in great detail the finer qualities of each. He truly was torn.

Lauren wanted Cameron to share his feelings with her but he didn't know how. These are things men learn over time; it's not a quality that most men possess. They are great at knowing how to "hunt, provide and protect."

Cameron's thoughts:

June 16, 2005

"Wow...I've been busy doing other things when I was supposed to be writing this...that... ya know. I miss cami and Jaclyn from ad design. Gah... and what two lovely young ladies. *Sigh*

I think I'm going to miss school. I thought that once I graduated, I wouldn't be able to see my friends every day. That was a bullshit thought. The only problem is that some of my friends will disperse after summer is over, so that they can further their lives. Then... I'll both miss and be happy for them at the same time. I'll still keep in contact, though, I'm sure. And if I don't...tough titty. This is life.

I've stumbled across the thought, with the brainwaves of another, of getting an apartment with Tyler. Like...the one I met freshman year that I completely idolized as the perfect personality of what punk-rock should be. Anyways, nikki is about to be kicked outta her place in the somewhat near future, as well. Should not the three of us combine forces and get an apartment together?

I think it'd be pretty sweez. We'll simply live together, hang out mildly often, and help each other stay alive.

Well, I have to go and...uh...prepare. Yes, prepare! The night is young... and I'm growing old. I'm 730ish days away from being two decades old. Shit.

Okay, champagne wishes et caviar dreams.

cameron."
10:07 pm

Oh how I wished this plan had taken place!

JUNE 17, 2005 (MYSPACE)

"...Agony is a sort of desolate place. Yet...no matter where one turns, they will find they're ever alone. There is a heavy depression that combs the ground; a sort of matting that gives a glint of anxiety with every step. Agony is a place of broken glass, shattered mirrors, weeping willows, misfired handguns. A place that is always welcoming when everything in the world has vanished in font of you. Nightmares through daydreams. Whispers through shouts. Vacant apartments. There is no sunrise or sunset, but instead, a sort of dim glow thought overcast skies. All inhabitants dress in rages, and the sound of crying babies is frequently heard, echoing in the background. Pastel shades of earth-tones keep the enthusiasm dulled, whole the soft murmur of thunder breaks through seemingly endless sound of eternal sleep. This wasteland of broken promises and harsh realities is our setting for the rabbit and the ferret.

The ferret in opposition to the rabbit is used to Agony. He's seen tragedy, witnessed heartbreak, and suffered from despair. He know that, in such fields, the only way to avoid being the prey of all the dismal disappointments of the world is to be the predator. He steals, cheats, flatters, lies and breaks hearts in order to keep his already battered emotions stable. Every day is just another lie; every individual just another threat.

The ferret's defense, though sometimes brutal, is well earned his rejection of the rabbit seems intense; almost black-hearted. The rabbit has now been properly and unexpectly introduced to Agony. The ferret feels regret for what had to be done. Though not the first victim of the ferret's insecurity, the rabbit realizes that life is honest... and that even if the honesty hurts, it is always for the best. The rabbit is now enlightened, though still heartbroken. The ferret is now free from the babble of nonsense and bogus philosophy. Neither is happy about the outcome, but in Agony, both must feel the pain as they navigate down the road of broken glass, towards a new place in themselves.

Happy ending? Not quite. The rabbit is able to overcome the pain and eventually shrugs off the burden. The ferret, however, ponders the emotions of the rabbit. He questions every second of their time together, looking some way to mend the wounds inflicted. So... as the rabbit eventually navigates out of the mind-numbing conflict, the ferret remains in Agony, waiting for a new rover to eventually crush again. Self improvement lingers in his mind, but remaining in Agony only leads to his fated self destruction.

I am the ferret. Goodnight,

Cameron"
11:26 pm

I could tell from the Rabbit – Ferret blog that Cameron was starting to feel beaten down from outside sources (girlfriends perhaps?).

As for me, I was frantically going on job interviews but no one was offering me a job. I was ready to move if no one would give me a job.

JULY 2005

Cameron's thoughts:

July 2, 2005 (MySpace)

"I've decided to babble a smidge. Throughout the last few days I've been fired, bored, elbowed (numerous times), flattered, utterly pissed off, shot-down, blamed, blazed and wasted. I feel like such a pawn to life. But then...I've come to conclude that life shouldn't be compared to chess. It's more like checkers. Lots of single pieces...when you get to the end, you have to wait until the end of the board to find out how to get back where you came from, always one finds his/herself going ever onwards...there's an abundancy of red and black? Whatevskies.

So I haven't posted anything in quite a while. Alas, I have reason why tucked away. But seriously, I've just been sleeping a lot. It's as if work completely drained me...I didn't want to see people. I didn't want to go do anything...I just wanted to go to sleep in my fucking bed. And fuckall to the rest. Fuckin' bloody pieces... I made a picture of a fucked-up doll. If anyone's up to take a peeky, it's gonna be posted below. It kinda freaks me out if I look at it too long. Cause everybody must get stoned."

During the summer it was obvious that Cameron had returned to heavy drug use. He was very secretive about everything he did and quite frankly, we didn't push him about where he was going or what he was doing.

He was, by law, an adult now and still lived at home. Since

that was the case he did need to follow our rules because he lived there for free.

By July, he was without a job again and his Social Security payments had stopped when he turned 18 in May. He needed money in order to pay for car insurance and just to have money to go out with friends, so he needed to find another job.

Dan was pissed at Cameron for a multitude of reasons: drug use again, no job, being hateful, sleeping all day, etc. We wanted to see a change in Cameron but were not sure how that was going to happen.

***

I met Cameron at Dr. Zrnic's office for his monthly appointment. Cameron obviously had used meth before walking into the office, as he had the shakes. I noticed his hands trembling a lot while we were in the waiting room. I asked him about it and he just shrugged his shoulders.

I'm sure he knew full well why he had the shakes – meth. He probably smoked some right before his appointment, since we drove separately. I was so discouraged by his actions.

During my time with the doctor (after Cameron would see him), I expressed my concern that Cameron seemed more depressed lately. I mentioned that Cameron had been cutting the week before. That was usually a clue that a person was depressed.

He said he had already asked Cameron the litany of questions that determined if a person was depressed, and he said that Cameron had only two or three of the requirements that expressed depression.

To hell with that depression test! I was correct and I was told that he was fine.

His doctor also suggested Cameron stop taking Abilify, which was prescribed to level his emotions out. He said that Cameron needed to begin talk therapy again, with another therapist in place of taking Abilify.

I was in agreement but knew that Cameron wouldn't talk to a therapist. We had tried that for three years with several different mental health professionals and Cameron told them each the same lie: that he was fine.

Dr. Zrnic made another suggestion, which actually got the ball rolling in the right direction for Cameron; he suggested to Cameron that he might want to register for some college classes.

I shared all the results of the office visit with Dan, but he balked at the idea of college registration for some reason.

Cameron spent the night away from home that night. It seemed that visits to therapists or doctors always made him sad.

A note I made in my journal at the time:

> "I feel like maybe I should just leave everything! Just go back to NC with Cameron in tow. Dan's not happy, neither am I. Maybe he can come out after the house is sold. I don't know..."

On the last day of July, Cameron filled out an application to attend classes at NCTC, North Central Texas College, in Gainesville. He's ready to go to college now!

AUGUST 2005

We weren't enthusiastic about Cameron's sleeping all day, so we enforced a new rule that got him out of the house by noon; he was to look actively for a job. Of course, we didn't know what he did when he left the house. We found out later that he would go to his friend Zach's house and sleep there.

Dan and Cameron were arguing on a regular basis now. Cameron would say, "I hate you." Dan was not getting any respect from his stepson.

I discovered the following poetry Cameron had written, which illustrated his depression:

Denial is Hope.

I'm 18 years into it,

And I'm already sick of life.

I've seen enough...

And it makes me heart-broken

To keep living in this mess of a world.

If people are lame enough to kill over

Opposing religious beliefs,

What good am I?

I can't change anything.

So why live trying to?

Quitting was invented for the thoughtful...

There's nothing negative about it.

Other thoughts written on the same page:

> Once nothing exists,
>
> Everything is a happy memory.

Another:

> I don't want it anymore.
>
> Not your bullshit.
>
> Not your smile.
>
> Not your idiocy.
>
> Not you…
>
> > Let me take the wrong path.

***

Dan and I had a talk one day while I was at my computer.

He said, " I want you to promise that Cameron won't move back to North Carolina with us."

I was stunned by this and remember crying and saying, "What if something happened to Cameron? No, I can't promise that."

He was not thrilled with my response, but I pictured Cameron as being in some accident and then he would need to live with us so I could take care of him. It was just too much of a promise for me make about my son. (I would have dreams after we moved back to North Carolina that Cameron moved into our game room, which could have been a big bedroom. That promise continues to haunt me).

Dan left the next day (August 5) for Raleigh on another house hunting trip leaving Cameron and I alone with Sheila.

Cameron wrote this in his green journal sometime during the week:

> I'm totally going to college soon. Given, it is NCTC... still. Fuckin' college, man. Where did all those years go? Crazy aging process we humans have. Not a ton of animals live to be 100. I wonder what tortoises must think as they finally become over-the-hill at age 150. Wow that topic changed rather quickly.
>
> Anyways, I'm all ancy like a schoolgirl to start at NCTC. What fun, what knowledge, what mayhem will I stumble upon? I finally get to start over again. What greater honor is there than a resurrection? Finally an open window to meet new people, learn new things, and to truly be who I am without having to regret my actions.
>
> Another thing that is "tickling" me ; it kicks ass being 18. Its as if in all the previous years, I was kicked aside by older people. My opinions and outlooks constantly mocked. I'm free now...you may know more than me & have lived longer, but that doesn't make you wiser (wisdom – the application of knowledge). So fuck you if you disregard my input, but it will always be there...never unspoken, never sugar-coated. I'm open to new ideas...are you?

***

Monday August 8 - Cameron finally landed a part-time job at Wolf Camera but in a location he hated – Grapevine Mills Mall. He was scheduled to start on Wednesday. Cameron's friend Zach came over and was very happy for Cameron.

We thought he'd be excited to finally work at a camera store. He had tried to get a job at Wolf Camera for more than a year, but at the store closer to home in Flower Mound, so he didn't show much excitement.

I offered to help Cameron get his uniform together for his new job. (I knew he wouldn't do it himself nor did he have the money. We really wanted him to work again and have some purpose in his life). I went to Kohl's, which was close to home and my go-to for clothes.

Cameron texted me to find out where I was and I texted back, "Kohl's." He showed up shortly after to ask about dinner.

> "Hi mom! So it's Tuesday. Are we eating Chick-fil-A tonight?" (There was a family special on Tuesdays at Chick-fil-A and we usually took advantage of it).
>
> "Sure. Aren't you going to thank me for buying you clothes to work in?" I was a bit annoyed that he assumed I would take on this task for him.
>
> While giving me a sideways hug, he said, "Thanks Mom."

That was to be the last hug I would get from my son.

He left the store in a hurry. He called me while I was still shopping and we agreed to meet at home to eat our Chick-fil-A meal together.

He ate quickly and left again. He was very agitated and excitable that day. I'm guessing his meth use was to blame.

***

Wednesday August 10 - Today was Cameron's first day at his new job at Wolf Camera. He went to work at 10:00 a.m. but sometime, during the day he also did a meth run to Garland per Lauren and Kelly who went along with him (this was shared with me later on by Lauren).

Bonnie, my good friend from Florida, was visiting me for a quick one day/one night stay. Before Cameron left for work, he graciously thanked Bonnie for his graduation gift. He was always polite and thanked people for gifts. I even had him write thank you notes for gifts received from relatives.

Bonnie and I went to Ikea in Frisco and spent most of the day there shopping. When we got home later that afternoon, we were sitting outside on the patio when Cameron stopped by the house.

He announces, "I'm hungry. What's for dinner?"

"Bonnie and I are going to dinner at Ana Mia's. You're welcome to join us."

"Nah. That's okay. I'll go find some food with friends."

Bonnie and I headed for Ana Mia's, my favorite Mexican restaurant in Flower Mound.

Cameron called at 11:00 pm to say he needed to give Nikki a ride home at midnight and he would be home after that. He called because his curfew was 12 midnight.

I went to bed leaving a light on by the stairs for him.

An entry in Cameron's green journal during this time period reads:

Still Thursday morning...

I swear...karma's kicking my ass. I wrote Lauren a note because it's hard for me to talk about the way I feel about things...so I get to the end, drive to her house, pick a flower from the neighbor's yard, and go up to her car to place her presents inside. As soon as I try to open the locked door, I feel sprinkles. Then it gets harder...then harder...in seconds it's pouring. I let the letter and flower stay sticking out the door, and walked back to my car through the curtain of individual droplets

Even though a desperate attempt at saving myself but a fraction of a point, nature foils my plans. It's almost as if I can't catch any relief...but that's bullshit, because...great. my pipe just broke. I need to pause for reflection now.

When I got up at 3:30 a.m., I noticed the light had been turned off meaning Cameron had come home as he said he would. I was up at that time since I took Bonnie to the airport for her flight home.

We were in the kitchen making tea when Cameron showed up at the back door around 5:00 am. The back door was mostly glass so I saw him standing there. He scared me – he looked like a ghost standing there. He was wearing jeans and a black t-shirt so he blended in with the darkness of the early morning.

He wanted me to unlock the door for him since I was right there.

"Wow! You scared me!" I noticed his hair and clothes were wet.

"Why are you wet?"

"I was out skating and then went over to Lauren's house to leave her a note. I tried calling her but her mom said I couldn't talk to her since it was so late. So I decided to write her a note. I wanted to put it in her car but the door was locked so I left it on the windshield. Then it started raining. I hope the note's okay."

"It probably will be alright." I then said to Cameron, "Dan is coming home today."

His response, "Not already."

"You need to go to bed since you've got to go to work again in the morning. You need to get some sleep."

Cameron said, "I have plenty of time to sleep since I don't have to be there till 3:00."

He went straight upstairs. This was to be the last time I saw Cameron alive and that was our last conversation.

Bonnie and I left for the airport at 5:35 a.m.

AUGUST 11, 2005

I RETURNED HOME AROUND 6:30 in the morning and decided to lie back down on the bed. It was cool with the ceiling fan blowing on me; it was a hot August morning after all. I fell back to sleep easily. I was awakened when the phone upstairs started ringing at 7:00 a.m. This was Cameron's landline. It stopped ringing but started up again a few minutes later.

This time I woke up angrily and was determined to tell whoever was calling to stop! I got up and started to make my way upstairs. Up the beautiful winding staircase that made me fall in love with this house, across the loft, which was my "office," and into the hallway, which lead to Cameron's room. No doubt the phone would be in his room.

But as I walked through the loft, I see the attic stairs are down. I thought, "That's odd. Why would the stairs be down?"

As I get closer, I see Cameron's feet hanging down out of the opening.

(Pause – as I have to relive this horrifying time in my life again for you, the reader).

I look up and see he has hung himself! I go up the pull down stairs to where I can get a hold of him and pull up on his body to try and loosen the rope from his neck.

I screamed, "Cameron! Please don't leave me! I'll do anything! Please don't go! Please!"

August 11, 2005

I'm frantic! What do I do to save my son?

I quickly thought of what I needed to do next – "Get something to cut the rope and hopefully save Cameron. If I go downstairs to the kitchen to get a knife, it will take too long. Is there something up here I can use? Yes! There are scissors in the craft room!" It was located right behind the stairs.

I maneuvered my way around the stairs and came back with orange handled scissors. I went up the stairs and cut the rope that was binding my son's neck.

Cameron fell to the floor – about a 5-6 foot drop. I thought, "Great. If he wasn't dead already, he surely is now since I made him fall so far."

He was slumped in the hallway, half in his bathroom doorway, and half in the hall. I tried to straighten him out. He didn't look good. I thought to myself, "What do I do now?

Call 9-1-1!"

I got the phone off Dan's desk in the game room and dialed 9-1-1.

> I urgently said, "Hello. I just found my son and he has hung himself."
>
> "I'm sorry ma'am. What's your address?"
>
> I responded, "3309 Pecan Meadows Drive in Flower Mound."
>
> "Do you know how to perform CPR?"
>
> "I learned a couple of years ago but..."
>
> "Don't worry ma'am, I'll lead you through it. Is your son laying flat?"
>
> "No, he's on his side, half in the bathroom and a hallway."

August 11, 2005

"See if you can lay him flat so you can open his mouth."

I put the phone down and struggled to move Cameron into a good position. Cameron was 6 feet tall and weighed around 200 pounds – he wasn't little.

Somehow I managed to get him flat. He was lying mostly on his bathroom floor. I went around him into the bathroom by the tub so I could reach his mouth.

Back to the phone, I told the responder, "Okay. I have him flat. Now what?"

"Open his mouth and breathe into it so you can see his chest rise."

I did so and saw my only child's chest rise. But he did not breath on his own.

"I did but he's still not breathing. What do I do?"

"I want you to go unlock your front door so EMS can get in when they arrive. I've already called them. After you do that, come back and continue mouth-to-mouth resuscitation."

I told him, "Thank you" and hung up the phone.

I ran downstairs and unlocked our front door. EMS arrived within minutes. Several of them rushed upstairs to work on Cameron. They moved him to the loft area because there was more room to work there.

I had no idea what they were doing. I watched them as they were preparing to take him to the emergency room. I was sitting

August 11, 2005

on the couch in the loft dumbfounded by everything that had transpired and looking down at Cameron while they worked on him.

I finally asked, "Do you have to take him to the ER? It seems unnecessary at this point."

I remembered how much Cameron hated going to the hospital in the EMS vehicle after his seizure. I knew he'd hate to find out that he went in another one.

No, I didn't know if he was dead or alive at this point.

"Yes ma'am, we do" was the response I received.

By then, there was a detective downstairs and he had let Lauren inside. I was angry when I saw her because I wanted to put the blame on her. She was sitting at our formal dining room table crying and confused. I don't know how she found out about Cameron.

EMS was taking Cameron to the Lewisville Medical Center and they were hurrying. Maybe they had a faint heartbeat – I didn't know – no one told me.

My brain was telling me, "They're taking him to the hospital because they think they can save him. Why else would they do that?"

Lauren and I watched as they wheeled Cameron out on a stretcher into the hot summer air. They were giving him oxygen.

They put him in the back of the EMS vehicle and left for the hospital.

I had softened towards Lauren by then because she was so

August 11, 2005

distraught. I told her I was going to the hospital and she left to go home.

> The detective asked me, "Do you want to ride along in the unit with your son?"
>
> "No. I need to get some things to take with me to the hospital."

I was thinking that Cameron would be okay, and since I'd be there waiting, I would need a sweater. I remembered the hospital was cold when we went after Cameron's seizure. I put a sweater and some jeans in a small bag.

I also called Dan from the bathroom while I was getting ready, to let him what was going on. Dan was due to return home that day and had already left for the airport. I told Jon, Dan's friend that he was staying with, about Cameron and said that Dan needed to come home ASAP. I didn't say whether he was dead or alive because I didn't know.

Before I got ready to leave, I went upstairs after they've taken Cameron out to look around his room for - I don't know for what. I saw a green, felted journal that I hadn't seen before, so I grabbed it to look at while waiting at the hospital, but when I saw the detective, I gave it to him for possible clues as to why Cameron would end his life.

> *(My heart still beats wildly while writing and reading this.)*
>
> I headed to my car in the garage to drive to the hospital and the detective who had been so caring during the whole ordeal said, "Ma'am, you're not driving anywhere. You're in shock. Can someone else take you?"

"No, my husband is out of town."

"Then we'll have a police officer drive you. Is that okay?"

I nodded in agreement.

Before I left, I remembered that Sheila was somewhere around. Since the detective was staying behind, I told him, "Please be careful to not let our dog out of the house."

"Don't worry. I'll leave from the garage so she won't get out." He was a very nice man.

On the way to the hospital, I was dazing out the window and I think I sat in the front seat.

The officer asked me, "Do you have family who can meet you at the hospital?"

"No. My husband is returning from a trip and the rest of my family all live in North Carolina."

"What about a friend?"

Mentally, I started going through my friends who would and could meet me at the hospital. I was thinking to myself, "I could ask Micki but she's just had a baby so she can't and plus she lives kind of far away."

Honestly, all the friends that I would want in a situation like this lived in North Carolina but finally, I thought about Mary Jane. Thinking to myself again, I said, "Mary Jane! She would come if she can. I'll call her."

I knew Mary Jane from our car club. She and her husband

had become friends of ours.

    Calling Mary Jane, I tried to explain what was going on.

    "Hi Mary Jane. This is Carolyn. Cameron has hung himself and I need someone to meet me at the hospital in Lewisville. Dan is on his way home from North Carolina but I don't know when he'll be back. Can you meet me? A police officer is driving me now."

    Mary Jane responded, "Oh honey! Yes I'll be there as quick as I can. I'm so sorry."

    "Thanks Mary Jane."

    The officer, satisfied that I had taken care of that task, then asked me if there was someone I should call and tell what had happened. I'm thankful for him leading the way because I couldn't think of anything. I was totally in shock.

    I called my mom at home in Raleigh. "Mom. Cameron has hung himself and I'm on my way to the hospital."

    I don't remember any other part of that conversation. I do seem to remember being upset and crying a bit. That's what happens when you share something dreadful with your mother. I only wish I had her with me with her arms wrapped around me.

    After what seemed like an eternity, we arrived at the hospital. It was only a six-mile drive but there was morning traffic to get through.

August 11, 2005

The officer dropped me off at the entrance to the emergency room and someone took me to a small room off to the side of the ER. It was in this room I spent a long period of time, first wondering if Cameron was dead or alive, and then having to make several difficult decisions.

Mary Jane arrived about 10 minutes later. She joined me along with a minister and the police officer who drove me to the hospital.

We sat and waited for the answer to the question: is Cameron dead or alive?

After, perhaps 30 minutes, a doctor came in and said sadly, "I'm sorry but we did everything we could. We couldn't revive your son. Do you want to go see him?"

You'd think I would have jumped at that question and said, "Yes!" but I hesitated. I asked Mary Jane, "Do I want to see him?"

"It's up to you."

I agonized over this and finally I determinedly said, "I'll regret it if I don't see him one last time."

I am so sad remembering this moment....

They led me over to where Cameron laid on a stretcher, next to a wall. He had a sheet pulled up to his mid chest and he had a breathing tube in his mouth. His hair was still slightly wet and curly from just hours before when he had been in the rain leaving Lauren a love note.

His eyes were not totally closed so I could see his brown eyes.

August 11, 2005

The pain in seeing your child lying dead, never to open those eyes again is more than painful – it's excruciating.

Mary Jane was there with me, and so was the doctor. I don't remember who else was there but it seemed like there was an audience for my last moments with my son.

I went over and ran my fingers through his hair and said, "I love you Cameron. You were my best friend." and I just looked at him, still in disbelief that he was gone.

> *As I relive this, I am crying remembering that was the last time I saw my son. There are many days following that dreadful day that I don't remember, but this part I do – clearly.*

When I found him, I had lots of time with him, or so it seemed. I gave him mouth-to-mouth, moved him around and smelled his final scents. I remember that he had urinated so his jeans were wet (I've learned that's common for someone who has hung themselves). I could taste the taste from his lips for a very long time. It was a sweet taste, but remembering the urine smell was not pleasant.

> They led me back to the little room for more difficult decisions. One that I made, I still regret, "Do you want your son to be an organ donor?"

I shared with Mary Jane that Cameron and I had never talked about that. Who does with their child?

> I ultimately said, "No. We never talked about it so I don't know his feelings about it."

Now I know Cameron would not have cared.

August 11, 2005

Then there was the question of burial or cremation. Really? I had to make these decisions about my now dead son? Really?

They said I did not have to decide then but I would have to soon. Also, which funeral home did I want them to take Cameron to after the Coroner's office. I had no idea! That's something I would have known if I was in Raleigh, since I grew up there and went to funerals of friends and relatives.

However, I had not gone to any funerals since living in Texas. The minister said there was a funeral home in Flower Mound. That was fine with me.

Actually, I think I didn't have to decide right then, but would have to in the near future.

They were preparing to take him to Fort Worth to the Coroners office for an autopsy.

That was the longest hold up – waiting for the Coroner's office to come pick him up. I believe I had to sign a paper before they'd let me leave. I really wanted to get out of there!

The coroner finally arrived, the paper was signed, and Cameron was released. It was time for me to go home; not stay in the hospital with Cameron as I had hoped and planned for. He was not supposed to die!

Mary Jane got her car and pulled around to pick me up. I asked if she'd stop at a Chick-fil-A on the way home. As we went through the drive-thru, I ordered a gallon of sweet tea and a Chick-Fil-A biscuit, because surely I was hungry. I only took a couple of bites of the biscuit at home. Grief and shock takes away all hunger pangs.

We also stopped so Mary Jane could put gas in her car. I called Mom again while waiting for her to finish with the gas.

August 11, 2005

During that time, I had first called her and then, she had called all my sisters and they were at her house. I spoke to them all and each one was so pitiful crying. Oh my god - why was this happening?

We made it back to the house and it was so quiet. Usually there was music drifting down from Cameron's room.

I thought, "Where's Sheila?" but she was in the guest bedroom behind a closed door. She was happy to be out and with me.

Mary Jane and I talked a little more freely now. The detective had given Mary Jane a report that needed to be filled out. She asked me the questions, and I dutifully answered them. It was probably a criminal type report. This was much easier with my friend asking me than someone I didn't know.

Since Cameron was suppose to be at work at 3:00, I asked her if she'd call and tell them that he wouldn't be in. That was a difficult call for her to make and it was even harder for the manager who took the call.

I learned that he quit soon after his death. Cameron had worked there only one day. I went in to see the girl he worked with a few months after Cameron's death. She said she was shocked when she heard he had died. She remembered him as a sweet kid and she really enjoyed talking with him that day.

Mary Jane stayed with me until Dan's plane got in. He called around 1:00 when he was at the airport and Mary Jane drove to pick him up.

The poor guy didn't know for the longest time whether Cameron was dead or not. I had forgotten to share that with him when he called from the airport.

Mary Jane talked to Dan outside before she headed home.

She was probably filling him in on everything. She certainly was my angel that day.

While they were outside and I was finally alone, I sat on the couch rocking myself and squeezing my arm so tight with my hand that I left bruises. I was in such disbelief; I guess I wanted to see if I was alive.

Phone calls started coming in that afternoon from family and friends as word got out. Dan took all the calls. People wanted to come by but he told them all, "No". I'm not sure why but that's what he felt needed to be done.

I did allow Kelly and her Aunt Paula to come over the next night. I remembered how I was talking in third person like none of it happened to me. Paula was surprised how calm I was. I was in shock – that's why.

> Kelly told us, "I knew it was Cameron when I heard the sirens from the fire station near our house yesterday."

How did she know that? Because she was the last person Cameron spoke to on the phone that morning. No, I have not been told what was said.

I tried several times to let Cameron's stepmom and sister know about Cameron, but I had a very hard time getting in touch with them. When I did finally talk to Nannette, she screamed. Ultimately they blamed me for his death. The Blame Game – it's sinful.

The Flower Mound Funeral Home was very nice about dropping off papers that needed to be completed or signed. They were easy to work with and Dan dealt with the funeral home requests for the most part.

August 11, 2005

I wrote Cameron's obituary for the Raleigh newspaper. I also had to plan two memorial services, one in Flower Mound for all of Cameron's friends and ours and one in Raleigh for our relatives and friends who lived in North Carolina.

Cameron died on Thursday so we held a memorial gathering at the funeral home on Sunday. His body was still at the coroner's office and even if it wasn't, I'm not crazy about open casket viewings. My policy is to remember the person alive and happy, not lying in a casket but I had many pictures of Cameron at the memorial.

Many people came that afternoon. Several of the kids got together and signed a guitar and gave it me in honor of Cameron. That was so thoughtful and kind. They made one tiny mistake – they misspelled Stephenson.

Lots of people like to brag about how many people came to a funeral. That's not important to me. What's important is to provide a space where everyone can mourn together and share memories of the person who died.

That was achieved at the memorial in Flower Mound. It was comforting to be able to provide that type of atmosphere for Cameron's friends.

I had friends from Nokia come to see us as well as friends from the TOWN group I belonged to; flowers arrived at the funeral home in Cameron's memory. There were so many peace lilies!

When it was almost time to go home, Cameron's favorite teacher and mentor, Magistra, showed up. She was very saddened by his death as well. I always liked her, as she was from North Carolina originally and she meant so much to Cameron.

August 11, 2005

With that behind us, we had to get ready to fly to Raleigh for a church memorial service on Wednesday at Hayes Barton Baptist Church. Dr. Hailey, the minister, was gracious and provided a heart-warming service for us.

On the plane flight back, I wrote details about Cameron's life for Dr. Hailey so he had something to go by. He did not know us intimately but he did marry Dan and I, which included Cameron eight years prior to this unfortunate gathering.

I remember on our journey back, we were in Austin waiting for a flight so Dan and I were killing time looking in the terminal's shops. One of the small shops had mood rings and Dan bought us each one.

The flight was terrifying for me. I was so afraid someone would talk to me. I didn't want to talk to anyone who didn't know what had happened to our family, so I stuck close to Dan the entire trip.

Dan and I stayed at Kristie and Kelly's house in north Raleigh. They provided the most comfort to me whenever I needed it.

> The day of the service I asked Kristie, "Which skirt should I wear?" Like anyone would notice.

Before the service in Raleigh, the family gathered in the church parlor. While we waited to go into the chapel for the service, Dr. Hailey came by to say hello and ask if we had anything else we wanted to add to the service, as well as to see how we were doing.

> I was standing there with Dan, Kristie, and Kelly when Mom came over and interrupted by announcing to Dr. Hailey, "Look at all beautiful

August 11, 2005

children" or something along that vein.

I felt it was totally out of place and said to her, "Not now Mom."

This was hurtful to her, as I had hoped it would be. It just wasn't the right time and place to make mention of <u>her</u> children while we were there for the death of my child, and her grandson.

For the longest time, I held a grudge against her for this interruption and for saying something so out of place. This year, I learned to master the art of forgiveness and I have forgiven my mother regarding her comment. I now realize she was probably nervous, since her grandson had died and this was her way to break the ice or to cover up her sadness.

I always loved the chapel where the service was held because it was so cozy feeling. I took Cameron to a Thanksgiving service there when he was six months old.

The service was perfect but I hardly heard a word of it because I kept my focus on the white orchid that Kelly's parents had sent for the service. I did not want to come unglued.

I requested a copy of the service from Dr. Hailey, so I could read it. He obliged and mailed me a copy.

Kristie created a beautiful memorial card for the service. We had many friends and family attend, but it was mostly a blur.

While we were in Raleigh, Dan showed me a house that he thought would be perfect for us when we move back. We signed a contract on August 19 to have a house built in quiet Youngsville on a heavily wooded lot.

We flew back to Texas the next day with a new future in front of us sans our son, Cameron.

REGRETS, WISHES, AND RECOMMENDATIONS

F OR MY CONCLUSION, I will share what people have and will ask me.

First, do you think there's anything else you could have done to save your son? It seems I/we did everything we could do within our power and means. The one thing I didn't try was moving with my son. That still haunts me.

But deep in my heart I know that since Cameron was an addict, he would have found the means to continue his meth habit. Sending him to rehab over and over wasn't an ideal situation either. Further, he was an adult at the time and had the power to make his own decisions.

I do wish I had been able to tap into his trust fund to provide more funds in order to continue his therapy with the one psychologist he liked, as well as his psychiatrist. They seemed to get through to him but I was not the keeper of his trust fund (a mistake on my ex-husband's part) so we provided what insurance provided us – the usual six visits per therapist.

My wish naturally is that my son was still alive and struggling with being a topnotch photographer. He'd have a romantic interest that could help with the marketing aspect of getting jobs. She would be pestering him about marriage and having kids. They'd live in a different state, but we would see each other on a regular basis. We'd all be happy.

I think I'll dream on that one night soon, to see the happiness on everyone's faces. I don't generally allow myself the luxury of imagining, "what if" because it doesn't help matters or change anything.

Today, I help many others with their grief of losing loved ones, not just by suicide but any type of death. I've learned that the way someone dies really doesn't affect the extreme loss that we feel afterward.

Yes, an unexpected death is earth shattering, but so is losing a child or watching your spouse die from a disease. Your future has been stripped away with that person and the pain can be so unbearable that you consider ending your own life.

The nonprofit I started, The Shore Grief Center, is for those who have experienced a death and are having a difficult time moving forward. They can see others attending our groups, who have survived a death and realize they can laugh again and be able to put one foot in front of the other. We form bonds and help each other through trying moments in life. Hopefully, one day they can help someone else with a death, too.

I have helped many grieving adults, teens and children, and they have helped me, too. I never pictured this role when I was considering a career for myself in my 20s. I wanted to be a fashion designer, but that dream drifted away. I then set my sights on being a fashion buyer for a chain of stores but that didn't fabricate either. I had a series of jobs in office settings, which were easy for me. However, when I had to raise my son on my own, I was determined to do more with my abilities and returned to school. I achieved the goal of earning a BA in Communications when Cameron was 9 years old.

I discovered my love of research and writing, while at North Carolina State University and I have used my talent to share my stories with others. Yes, I could go back to college and earn another degree, but I am fulfilled now by helping others in the method that was offered to me after my son's death.

I hope to continue writing, as I'd like to share my recovery story as well as other stories within me. However, I need to also be available for my husband and family as well as continue to scratch my travel itch.

RECOMMENDATIONS FOR OTHER PARENTS

This is a hard one for me, as I feel like a failure since my son died but I recommend that if you can stay strong mentally and financially, continue the fight of finding what will cure the mental illness or drug addiction your child may be experiencing.

Keep in the back of your mind, at all times, that when we're born we are given the power of free will. Every one of us, the power of making good or bad choices, and those deeply conflicted with events surrounding their lives can choose to end their life. Suicide has been an option for many since the beginning of mankind.

Yes, it's taken me many years to be so gallant and say such things, but I know it's the truth and wish others would realize it as well.

How to stop suicides? Be aware of the signs of depression and help those individuals get the help they need. Get them on the path to recovery before drugs and alcohol take over. Make that call for them and stand in the way of a potential suicide. Do what you can to help.

Realize that not everyone can be saved. Many are great actors and you may not see the signs in them as clearly as you can in others. Don't beat yourself up if you miss those signs.

Everyone should be vigilant to those around them. Not just your child, but perhaps your boss has been depressed for longer than 2 weeks. Have a conversation with them.

"Joe, I've noticed that you've been really down for a long time. I'd like to help you find someone to talk to about your problems."

You can then call your Employee Assistance program, or local mental health department to get help for them.

If it's gone further don't be afraid to ask more questions. If you sense they are considering ending their life, ask this question....

"Do you have a plan to end your life?"

Most likely, they will tell you "no" but this opens the door for an open conversation for them to share what's going on in his or her life. Offer to make an appointment with a therapist and go with them if they would like.

I had to ask someone that recently. She said, "No" but I am very aware that parents whose children die are very susceptible to suicide. Many of us, in order to get out of the daily agony of loss, start to think about how we can be with our child again. Of course, that's not logical but neither is the death of a child.

Be vigilant to those around you and offer help. Make the calls for them if necessary.

In this new age of rampant violence and seemingly lack of concern for our fellow neighbors and co-workers, take time to say "hello" or offer help if they need it. We must get our nation back on track and care about each other, and not so much ourselves.

I wish you, the reader, peace in your journey of recovery, for guidance with your child, or with helping others.

Peace

HOW TO MANAGE GRIEF

I can only give a parent's perspective on how to deal with grief after a loved one dies so I surveyed several teens, now young adults, I know to get their ideas on the following questions:

How long was it before you felt almost back to normal?

They all responded, "Forever changed."

Was there someone who helped you through the tough times?

- » Friends, helped. Two of them have passed away since my first deaths (that he/she experienced).
- » Ex husband
- » Family and friends

If no one helped you through your grief, what did help you?

- » Honestly I haven't let myself grieve. I know it's been over a year, but it's just something I choose to do and now I'm paying for it.
- » My friend helped me

» I was 10 when my father passed, once I had spent more time without him than with him, it oddly made it much easier to know I could keep going.

Did you receive help at some point from one or any of the following?

57% said a therapist or other mental health professional helped

43% said a grief support group

14% said Church

28% mentioned that friends, family and personal growth help. Another stated that close friends of the lost loved one helped.

Did you turn to drugs?

Most responded yes to using anti-depressants or illicit drugs.

One admitted that he became an alcoholic and drug addict while at college but has since changed.

Share your recommendations for today's teens who are grieving the death of a loved one.

Speak to your friends and take comfort in them. Everyone needs time to themselves and private time is good. Too much inward time and you turn to things that aren't people. The interaction with people becomes just as stressful as the ordeal itself.

Try to hang on. It gets less painful.

This is something that's really hard. I made the mistake of letting myself not feel the things I needed to feel and that wasn't healthy. If you've lost someone close to you please go seek some sort of therapist. Don't wait to get help when you're at rock bottom.

I still have yet to figure out how to overcome the pain but I can definitely assure that the pain does not last forever. It's important to talk to someone whether it's a therapist, a friend, or even journaling.

Trying to numb your feelings with drugs doesn't help things; it only prolongs the inevitable. Eventually you have to face your demons. Once you do, you'll be better for it.

Talk it out. Reach out to family and friends. Don't ever forget how lucky you are to have known such a great person. Don't ask why or what could have been done. This isn't a punishment; it didn't happen for a reason, it's just cold unforgiving statistics. You will be okay.

Seek out help, don't be afraid to talk about it, and remember it takes time.

***

It is terribly difficult to continue life as you knew it before your friend or family member died but do persevere. No, we will never be the same but changed in a way in which to help others who may experience something similar in the future.

You can be there for them. Make recommendations because it's difficult to know what to do when you're grieving. Tell them what you did when you faced grief head on.

The object is not let grief turn into depression which some will find solace with alcohol and drugs. We know that is not the healthy way to manage grief.

If you find yourself feeling so depressed that you don't want to get out of bed or just drag through the day, ask for referrals of therapists in your community. There is nothing to be embarrassed about seeking this type of assistance. I saw a therapist before my son died because life was so stressful for me. I also saw one after his death. They both helped me face my grief.

I also found comfort in grief support groups. Everyone shared how he or she felt or what helped them during their intense periods of mourning. You will find a glimmer of hope and will want to carry on because you see that others have survived and so can you!

Grief can swallow up a soul. I've witnessed it more than once now that I am more aware of deaths in our community via my nonprofit, The Shore Grief Center. I've attended funerals of teens who died by suicide and soon after a friend will loss hope and die by suicide as well.

This also happens when parents experience the death of a child of any age. We also hear of married couples dying just months apart.

Grief is powerful but so is support. Please seek out support for yourself or someone you love.

DISCOVERIES AFTERWARD

I DISCOVERED THIS VERY long, depressing poem by Cameron's computer when I was finally strong enough to clean up his bedroom:

Something Wicked this Way Comes

To have so many things I want to say,
but be at a loss of words.
The thoughts I wish to preach
are thoughts that people have heard.

On warm summer nights,
especially of late,
I've pondered the thought of death
and whether I want to wait.

But I think I've become somewhat timid
in the proceedings of my "crime."

Maybe I'm simply procrastinating,
waiting for a better time.

"No better time than the present,"
people like to say.
Tomorrow's worthless agenda
has proven it to be this way.

So I write with pen and paper
the issues that I've thought.
But nothing seems to cheer me up:
my emotions are distraught.

I wish that all my melancholy
thoughts and true desires,
would be carried away on heavy wings
of a raptor that never tires.

To say "farewell forever"
to the treacheries of yore,
and then letting something blossom;
something to adore.

But that's a dream, a fairy-tale;
nothing tangible or true.

so for now I'll sit in sadness,

for there's nothing else to do.

The sun will rise, then later set.

My life is but a jest.

Something kill me soon, I bet of thee...

to put my presence to rest.

love,
Cameron

FROM CAMERON'S FRIENDS....

L AUREN HAD A very good friend, Taryn, who allowed me to interview her in 2011. She was living in Boston at the time and I was there for training on how to help grieving children who have lost someone to suicide. The interview was very informative.

Following are some quotes from Taryn:

"Cameron was really good at helping people focus and helping people calm down and realize there are other things to be concerned with."

She also said that Cameron helped her when her grandmother died.

She continued with more on Cameron, "I think Cameron was such an influential human being. It blows my mind how many people he touched. Good and bad. It's kinda crazy to look back at that. How even though it was a huge sacrifice how he really got people to look at life, pay attention. Really change. I saw a lot of my friends really turn their lives around."

Next she shared, "But what I do want to say to you is that you really did raise an incredible person. You really did. For the short period of time that I knew him, for the short period of time that all my friends knew him, they were all inspired. I can not tell you how many of us realized our creative abilities. I don't know if it was the time of our lives, the age that we were or the people that we met."

She goes on to say, "I'll never forget Cameron. And the reason I won't is I'll never forget how happy he made so many people. I think underneath he wanted to be happy. That comfort of depression is so great." I shared his diagnosis of major depression and poly substance abuse. Taryn said, "So when you're depressed, that's a blanket, you just use it."

Taryn was ultimately very jealous of the relationship Cameron had with her best friend, Lauren. Taryn felt like Cameron stole her away from her.

***

There were many blog posts on Cameron's Xanga Site and his myspace page starting on August 12, 2005. I've included some that show how much Cameron was loved and admired:

"There will never be anyone like you my friend none will ever replace you. Your smile will forever frozen in my thoughts when we would joke around. You were always up for a joke...."

From Cameron's Friends....

"I'm sorry I never told you what a great friend you were to me. I will always remember the good time I got to spend with you and the late night/early morning conversations we had on AIM. I will miss you. Until we meet again..."

"...It felt like a joke, the Cam I knew would never abandon everyone like this, there was a lot of crying, A LOT....thank you for showing me how to just joke around and be the closest to happiness I'll ever be...I'll see you again, I love you..."

"...I feel like I should've know, like I should've said something... and I have to ask why? Just earlier that day the three of us were cuddling in your bed... chasing you through Lewisville, throwing fruit at your car...visiting you on your first day of the job you'd wanted for months...you picked me up from work at 12:30 in the morning...we had plans with Zach for the next day... It's just Lauren and myself now...no third, brilliant, witty, amazing amigo to make us giggle or to go camping with...."

"...You were a good friend that everyone loved and never stopped caring about it. From the group and myself, WE love you. And we will never stop..."

"...Your soul is a value...forget me not...No one will ever forget you...and I wish you hadn't walked away from your life, my friends are hurt... I am hurt..."

From Cameron's Friends....

"Your parents are busy moving now, back to North Carolina. I saw the big moving truck and the boxes outside of your house and it's as if everything is... final. what's done is done. And I will always miss you. You were an awesome friend, I'm sure you have gotten a lot of that. But it's true, you had a little bit more pizazz than everyone else. I think about you all the time and I will always. Everytime, you bring a smile to my face. R.I.P. thanks for all that you were." (posted 7/28/2006)

"We used to get huge packages of pineapple and go to the pond near my house and sit and eat pineapple while we laughed at the ducks."

Me and Bob Dylan. (posted February 21, 2005 on MySpace)
So long honey, babe.
Where I'm bound, I can't tell.
Goodbye's too good a word, babe.
So I'll just say fare thee well.
I ain't saying you treated me unkind.
You could have done better, but I don't mind.
You just kinda wasted my precious time.
But don't think twice, it's all right.

RESOURCES

American Alliance for Grieving Children – information on how to help grieving children and teens https://childrengrieve.org

American Association of Suicidology – for suicide prevention www.suicidology.org/

American Foundation for Suicide Prevention – to find survivor support and more www.afsp.org

Save the Teens – for the signs of teen depression www.save-the-teens.com

The Shore Grief Center – for help after the death of someone vital in your life www.theshoregriefcenter.org

To purchase **"Save the Teens: Preventing suicide, depression and addiction"** visit www.save-the-teens.com

Cameron with Julia, his half sister; Washington NC, March 2002

Caddo Lake, TX, October 2001

Niagara Falls, Canada, June 2003

Resources

Dan, Carolyn, and Cameron, Christmas 2003

Cameron with his mom, Graduation Night, May 27, 2005

Muenster TX, November 2001

Senior Portrait, September 2004

Cameron Stephenson, Summer 2005

CPSIA information can be obtained
at www.ICGtesting.com
Printed in the USA
FFOW05n1942130517